LIFE OUT OF DEATH
in Mozambique

Elizabeth Carlos Sammut

From:-

Katie and Gordon

With our love in the

Lord Jesus.

C000039689

LIFE OUT OF DEATH
in Mozambique

Phyllis Thompson

HODDER AND STOUGHTON
LONDON SYDNEY AUCKLAND TORONTO

British Library Cataloguing in Publication Data

Thompson, Phyllis
  Life out of death in Mozambique
  1. Mozambique. Christian missions – history
  I. Title
  266′.00967′9

  ISBN 0 340 50275 4

Hodder & Stoughton Editorial Office: 47 Bedford Square, London WC1B 3DP.

Acknowledgements

My sincere thanks are due to Mr. Will Walker and the many other people, mainly connected with the Africa Evangelical Fellowship, who provided information and reminiscences for this book; to Miss Mollie Robertson for her assistance in typing the MS; to Pastor Martinho Campos for sharing his experiences (by interpretation); and to Scripture Gift Mission for so often making a room available for interviewing.

But primarily I am grateful to Mr. Gordon Legg himself, without whose records, reminiscences, and ever ready assistance in checking what had been written, the story of the growth of the church in Mozambique could never have been told.

Contents

Note

The story unfolded in this book spans more than fifty years (from 1935–1987), during which time many political changes occurred in Africa. Below is a list of some of the countries referred to.

Present Name	Old Name	Date of Independence
Angola (People's Republic of)	Portuguese West Africa Angola (Portuguese)	1975
Botswana (Republic of)	Bechuanaland	1966
Malawi	Nyasaland	1964
Mozambique	Portuguese East Africa Mozambique (Portuguese)	1975
Namibia	South West Africa	——
South Africa (Republic of)	South Africa (Union of)	1960
Swaziland	Swaziland	1968
Tanzania	Tanganyika Zanzibar	1961
Zambia	Northern Rhodesia	1964
Zimbabwe	Southern Rhodesia, then Rhodesia	1980

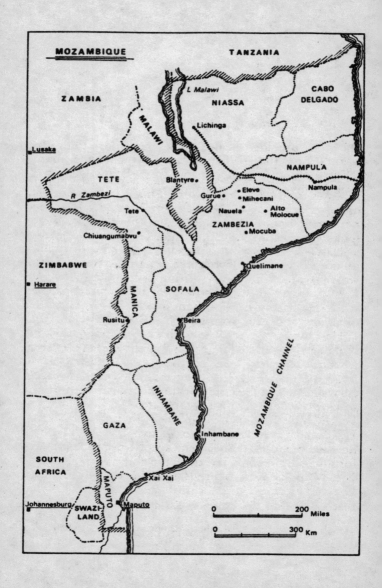

Prologue

The Green Line bus was due to leave in a couple of minutes, and as I peered through the traffic hurtling along Buckingham Palace Road to the crowded pavement opposite I wondered if the two men I was looking for would reach it in time. They were hurrying – at least, one of them was, pressing forward with a rather anxious expression on his face. The other, an African, was moving more slowly, lifting his feet cautiously, as though his shoes were too big for him, as indeed they were. He had borrowed them, not having a pair of his own, and they did not fit very well.

He always had trouble with his feet now, anyhow. Nineteen days forced march as a prisoner of the rebels in Mozambique had reduced them to pulp, and left his bones permanently stiff. The marvel was that he had survived at all, since he had been left for dead on the track. So when, after his escape, the Africa Evangelical Fellowship invited him to visit their International Headquarters in England to discuss the work for which he was responsible, one of the special needs he had was for suitable clothing. He knew the climate in the British Isles would be very different from that of Mozambique. Footwear proved to be a problem, and the shoes that fitted him best belonged to a fellow pastor in Maputo, who willingly lent them to him. And when he arrived at Heathrow his friend, the man even now hurrying on ahead of him, had provided him with a warm suit, a shirt and a tie.

So there he was, mingling rather awkwardly with the
pedestrians who passed him by without a glance, intent
on their own affairs, and I wondered if the apostle Paul
had appeared equally insignificant as he walked
through the streets of Corinth or Rome. For that
inconspicuous African, Martinho Campos, had an
influence among his own people comparable to that of
the apostles in New Testament days. His unceasing
itinerations over the length and breadth of northern
Mozambique had resulted in the formation of hundreds
of congregations, with baptised believers amounting to
160,000, with regular classes for women, Bible training
courses for men, and even day schools for children in
several places. In a country where literacy was around
20% such educational facilities were highly prized.

And all this against a background of nationwide
poverty and suffering for as long as he could remember.
The East African colony of Portugal in which he had
been born had been termed a province in 1951, and its
natural resources utilised for shipment to Portugal,
denuding it of its wealth. In the early 1960s nationalist
forces formed the Mozambique Liberation Front
(Frelimo) and guerilla warfare started, bringing terror
to the rural population. With the eventual triumph of
Frelimo over the Portuguese, Independence Day in
1975 ushered in an all-African Marxist Government,
which did not long remain unchallenged. Civil war was
started again, this time by a group named Renamo, the
National resistance movement of Mozambique. The
disruption of communication and the breakdown of the
economy resulting from the years of unrest, added to by
natural disasters of drought, flood and famine, had
brought about the conditions which placed Mozambique as the country with the highest rate of human
suffering in the world.

That the Church could even survive in such

circumstances was remarkable, but that it should grow and increase forty times its size to 140,000 in 25 years was little short of miraculous. Small wonder that the Africa Evangelical Fellowship, looking back over its own hundred years' history, felt that the time had come to reveal what God had been doing in Mozambique. Less was generally known about it than in any of the other countries where the Fellowship had been at work, yet nowhere was there a more moving or inspiring story to tell.

And the two men who had personally witnessed so much of it and been so vitally involved were even now turning the corner from Buckingham Palace Road to where the Green Line bus was standing. There was only a minute to spare. The traffic lights changed just in time for me to dart across the road and call out to them as they boarded it.

'Goodbye, Gordon! Goodbye, Martinho! Thanks for all you've told me! We'll be in touch!'

Then I went home with the notebook in which I had scribbled some of their reminiscences, pulled out the letters and reports, the booklets and magazines with which I had been supplied, and started to trace the story of how life came out of death in Mozambique.

1

God Called a Boy

Oxford Circus was as crowded as ever that autumn day
in 1935 as young Gordon Legg, immaculate with his
bowler hat and carefully rolled umbrella, walked
briskly along the street to enter D.H. Evans and take up
his usual position behind the counter in the men's
outfitting department. Everything was just as it had
been since he had started work as a salesman there four
years before, and there was no change in his manner or
appearance, either. He measured customers for suits
and coats, produced socks and ties to match, responded
courteously to the short-tempered and the critical,
generally behaving as one who has had it instilled into
him that 'the customer is always right'. No one would
have suspected that he had reached a crisis in his life,
and taken a step that he knew could lead him into an
entirely different world. That very day he had posted a
letter applying for admission into an establishment for
prospective missionaries, run by a Captain Godfrey
Buxton who had won a Military Cross in the First World
War and believed in training for work overseas being
tough. Gordon Legg had heard about it from a friend of
his who was already there, and his application to enter it
was the culmination of a series of apparently unrelated
incidents which had left an indelible impression on his
mind.

The first of these was when, as a twelve-year-old schoolboy who had just put his faith in Jesus, he had been sent by his parents to take a 22 lb parcel to the Post Office, addressed to his aunt in Swaziland. That act of practical participation in her work among Africans, simple as it was, gave him a sense of satisfaction and involvement which he would have found it hard to explain at the time. It was followed, three years later, by a memorable weekend when, after a meeting about Brazil in his church one Saturday evening, he was asked point-blank by the speaker, 'Have you ever thought of being a missionary?' The next day he was deeply stirred when listening to another missionary speaker, and on the Monday morning, before going to school, he was reading the Bible alone in his bedroom when he came to the words, 'Pray ye therefore the Lord of the harvest that he would send forth labourers into his harvest'. He stopped there, suddenly aware of the significance of what he had read. Ask God to send out workers... Was he to be one of them? The thought persisted through his years of apprenticeship in the men's outfitting trade, and when he heard that the firm in which he was working was opening a branch in South America he applied for a managerial post in it. It seemed like being a step in the right direction. However, although he was short-listed, he did not get the job, so that door closed. Then he met a missionary from Portuguese West Africa (now Angola) and made tentative enquiries about working with him. That did not materialise either, and at the age of twenty-three he was still commuting from Camden Town to Oxford Circus every working day, with no very clear sense of direction regarding Christian pioneer work overseas.

The challenge of the question put to him as a schoolboy had been answered. He had certainly thought of being a missionary, and was ready enough to take whatever steps were necessary to follow that calling. But the two abortive attempts to get moving had come to nothing, and he did not know what to do next when quite unexpectedly, through reading a magazine, the way was suddenly made clear.

The magazine was the periodical produced by the South Africa General Mission to which his aunt in Swaziland belonged.* The particular issue which reached him in the summer of 1935 announced that six young men, single, were needed to proclaim the Gospel in Portuguese East Africa.**

Single young men needed for Portuguese East Africa! As he knew, this was the country in which for years the society had been trying unsuccessfully to gain a foothold. There were S.A.G.M. workers in most of the other African countries south of the Equator, but none in the Portuguese colony on the east coast. Only a lonely grave marked the spot where one of the early pioneers had died. But now, it seemed, there were signs that an entry could be made and workers established within the territory. Gordon's heart had leapt as he read that call for single young men to take advantage of the opportunity, and it had been a matter of moments for him to decide he ought to be one of them. The next step would be to get the necessary theological training, and having heard about Captain Buxton's Missionary Training Colony he had written his letter of application and posted it that very morning.

'I hear there are more men wanting to enter the Colony than they are able to accept', he told his friend, a local policeman, who came round to his digs to see him that evening. Humanly speaking, there seemed no reason why his application should be more successful than anyone else's. But, as they agreed, if God wanted Gordon in that Colony, He could get him in. The urge

---

*South Africa General Mission, now Africa Evangelical Fellowship.
**Now the Republic of Mozambique.

to go forward, to prepare for missionary work, was too
strong to ignore. 'So let's pray about it.' And the two of
them knelt down beside the bed, and prayed most
earnestly that the Lord would incline the hearts of
Captain Buxton and his Council to open the door to
Gordon. But that was not all they prayed about.

The policeman had something on his mind, too. The
girl of whom he was becoming very fond was not a
Christian, and more than anything else he longed that
she should put her trust in Jesus Christ. So they pleaded
with God for that to happen as well. When they rose
from their knees, having shared each other's concerns, it
was with the consciousness of a deepening bond between
them, and they shook hands warmly as they parted at
the front door. Both prayers were answered, and they
rejoiced together.

In such ways links are formed that last for a lifetime.

The answer to Gordon's letter came within a few
days. It was courteous, if non-committal, but at any rate
the door was not closed. An appointment was made for
him to see a member of the Council. And so he set off for
the appointment after work, one evening in November,
praying silently and earnestly as he descended into the
Underground and travelled on the crowded train to the
station nearest to his destination.

He had rarely felt so inwardly tense, so apprehensive,
so conscious of his own inadequacy. What hope had he
of being accepted into a missionary training establishment when he was neither a medical man, a teacher, nor
an ordained clergyman? He had no professional
qualifications at all, being merely in trade, and he
wondered at his own temerity in applying. What
particular abilities had he to offer as a justification for
doing so, apart from superintending a thriving Sunday
School and taking part in open-air meetings? And in the
unlikely event of his being accepted, what would be
involved as he left the familiar security of his present

manner of life for the uncertainties of a missionary career in a strange land? As he walked along the deserted road to the Council member's house he suddenly felt the need to steady his mind. He came to a halt under a lamp-post, drew a deep breath, and pulled his Bible out of his pocket.

'Lord, speak to me through Your Word!' It was a prayer he often breathed quietly as he settled down for a period of Bible study, but this time it was different. He was approaching one of the most critical experiences of his life, on which so much seemed to depend, and he felt acutely a longing for reassurance. Without having any clear idea of where he could look for it, he opened the Bible at random. The leaves parted at 1 Chronicles 28:20, and his eyes fell on the words:

> Be strong and of good courage, and do it; fear not, nor be dismayed; for the Lord God, even my God, will be with thee; he will not fail thee, nor forsake thee, until thou hast finished all the work for the service of the house of the Lord.

It was all he needed. This was the direct answer to his urgent prayer. The God who is in the here and now, the great I AM, was speaking to him as surely as He had spoken to Solomon through the lips of his father David, thousands of years ago. 'Be strong and of good courage . . . for the Lord God, even my God, will be with thee . . .'

The whole incident took place in a matter of moments, but eternity was in it. Fifty years later Gordon remembered it as clearly as if it had been yesterday. He went on to the interview with a deep consciousness of God's presence, and it went well, even though the Council member said when it was over, 'Don't get too excited. We only accept one out of every five or six who apply'. As it turned out, he was the one. In due course he

was accepted for training, and enrolled for the next
session, due to begin in March.

So he started on the pathway that was to lead him to
Africa.

*   *   *

The Missionary Training Colony in Upper Norwood,
London, was not an impressive looking place. It
comprised some half a dozen army huts in a field. Here
thirty or forty young men lived together, slept
dormitory-style, twelve beds to a hut, ate the food they
had cooked themselves, washed their clothes in tubs in
the washroom, rising promptly at 6 a.m. for twenty
minutes of energetic physical exercises, followed by a
cold bath, winter and summer. 'Russian baths' the
young men called them – rush in and rush out. They had
been warned that the training, which was for pioneer
missionary work, would be tough, but that was what
most of them were prepared for. They wanted to be
good soldiers of Jesus Christ, and if that involved
enduring hardship, they were ready for it. Indeed, they
welcomed it – most of the time, anyway. They had little
leisure to stop and indulge any natural desire for ease
and comfort, for the days were full, with lectures every
morning and most evenings, and afternoons devoted to
what was termed 'practical work'. This included
carpentry and cobbling, gardening and hair-cutting,
maintenance to roads and buildings, lectures on tropical
medicine and 'How to reduce a language to writing'.
Two students at a time spent ten weeks at the Croydon
General Hospital, where they were allowed to attend
clinics, picking up what information they could about
the treatment of a variety of ills ranging from stomach
ache to fractured bones. On Saturday nights teams went
to the Thames embankment to try and help the down-
and-outs, while early mornings found others of them at

Piccadilly Circus, ready for the 'up-and-ins' emerging in various stages of inebriation from night clubs patronised by the wealthy. They must learn to reach out to all manner of people, particularly those who never went into churches.

It was an exhilarating life, especially when teams went off trekking for eight weeks each summer, pulling a hand-cart loaded with cooking pots and sleeping bags, and carrying their own packs on their backs. They went from place to place holding evangelistic missions or impromptu meetings on village greens, usually sleeping in church halls or in barns, where youthful high spirits sometimes erupted in practical jokes at the end of the day. Gordon joined in laughingly, on one occasion, as the team members decided something must be done to discourage the growth of moustaches among them. Paul Brand (later to become world famous as a hand surgeon, specialising in the treatment of leprosy) was the offender, sporting quite a flourishing tuft on his upper lip, so they got him down, though he struggled manfully, and shaved off, not all, but half of it.

'He took it all in good part', Gordon reported later. And Paul Brand got his revenge by refusing to shave off the other half, acting on the principle that:

> My face, I don't mind it,
>   For I am behind it.
> It's them that's in front gets the jar.

His tormentors 'got the jar' for the rest of the week every time they looked at him.

For all their occasional light-heartedness, the trainees in the Colony were very serious about their calling. It was expected of them. Without a deep-seated conviction that they were there by God's appointment, and that to Him they would have to give account in the day of reckoning, they would not have remained there long.

And they learned in a very practical way what it meant
to live by faith in Him to supply, not only their spiritual,
but their physical needs as well. It had been made plain
to them, right from the start, that the Colony had no
visible financial resources. Captain Buxton and his
colleagues looked to God alone for the means and the
money to support thirty-odd men in training for the best
part of two years. The support provided for the
necessities, not the luxuries, of daily living. There were
times when the words 'give us this day our daily bread'
took on a vital and practical meaning as it became
known that funds were very low, and there seemed no
prospect of income. One period in particular was
impressed on Gordon's mind. The situation was
unusually serious, and was saved by the arrival of a large
and unexpected cheque from Australia. It had been six
weeks on the way but arrived, as it were, in the very nick
of time. Faith and patience had been tested up to the last
minute, but the reward of joy and of strengthened
confidence was worth it. Gordon remembered that
incident as vividly as any of the Bible lectures he
attended, though his notebooks were full of what he
learned at them.

Most of the young men in the Colony were from the
British Isles, some of them destined to become leaders in
their respective fields – Bill Butler of Uganda, Jack
Dain, Bishop of Sydney, Philip Glass of the Evangelical
Union of South America among them. But there were
also some from Europe, Australia, Canada, India,
Africa.

Among this international group was a tall, loose-
limbed, auburn-haired South African with a genial
smile, named John Stafford. He and Gordon arrived at
the Colony on the same day, and it did not take them
long to discover that in addition to their Christian faith
they had something else in common. They both hoped
to go as missionaries to Portuguese East Africa.

It was heartening, almost exciting for them both to

meet. They got on well together right from the start, and shared confidences they would have hesitated to divulge to others. John admitted to Gordon one day how awkward he felt, coming from South Africa where the division between blacks and whites was so deep, to find himself sitting at table next to the dark-skinned man from India. He knew it was wrong, but the reaction was instinctive, due to his background. 'Please pray about it – I really need the Holy Spirit to change my attitude.' Such intimate confessions between them bound them together, and formed the basis of a friendship similar to that of David and Jonathan. It was the best possible relationship for the spiritual battles that awaited them.

The first ten months of training ended in December and the next two months were free. Some of the men got jobs, but Gordon decided that if he was going to a Portuguese colony he needed to understand Portuguese, both the people and the language. So he set about finding a way to go to Portugal.

It was not easy, for the Spanish Civil War was raging, but a friend introduced him to the captain of a cargo ship that was sailing from Barry Docks to Lisbon, and Gordon was registered as a seaman, since they took no passengers. He had a rough time of it, for they ran into a storm in the Bay of Biscay, the worst the captain had known in thirty years, and were tossed about for a week. Added to that, there were mines in the Bay and one ship, just ahead of them, struck a mine and went down. At one stage, when the storm was at its height, the ship reeled so badly that Gordon, alone in his little cabin, feared for his life. 'Oh, God', he prayed. 'Save me! Spare my life!'

Then he made a vow. He did not make many vows in his life, but this was one of them 'Oh, Lord! If you will spare my life now, I will serve you for ever'. It was an experience he never forgot. It was a vow he never forgot, either.

2

The Opening Way

'So now on a little elevated ground on the right bank of
the River Luenha there is a mud hut – our new home,
round in shape, after the manner of tribal buildings in
this area. There is a kitchen hut; the tent is pitched as a
store room; there is a hut for our cook and his wife; a hut
is being built for the other boys, and a place that will be
dignified by the name of a garage, which will also serve
as a workshop, for there is a lot of work to be done when
one is landed in the wilderness with a few tools, a few
boxes, and everything to make oneself.'

Gordon Legg and John Stafford were poring over a
buff-coloured, six-paged leaflet that they had looked at
several times before. It was the reproduction of a letter
written by Arthur R. Brown in October 1936, from the
first S.A.G.M. centre in Portuguese East Africa on a
tributary of the Zambeze River. It was illustrated by
small snapshots of a ramshackle raft ferrying a Ford
half-ton lorry across a river; a group of Africans in loin-
cloths and a European wearing a *terai* with the
inscription 'A.R.B. and some boys cutting a road
through the bush'; and a thatch-roofed hut under a tree,
with Mrs. Brown sitting in a deckchair by a table
covered with a white cloth, looking rather as though she
had been transported bodily from a tea-party on an
English lawn to the heart of Africa. The incongruity of

the scene was added to by the Ford lorry in the foreground.

The two young men scrutinised the pictures eagerly, noting every detail, and then went on reading the letter. In it Arthur R. Brown admitted to having felt some alarm at the prospect of encountering the herd of elephants which he had seen in the distance on several occasions. And there were other wild animals, too, less obvious to the eye, but even more to be feared. It was lion country.

'But one day we remembered that God had said "every beast of the forest is mine", so with the argument that they were His beasts, but we are His children, the fear has been taken away.

'We have a little garden in the wilderness. At present it has but a few cabbage plants and cucumber seedlings in it. It is circled by heavy footprints of the elephants, and there are two or three "marks of the beast" on the patch, but nevertheless it is preserved.'

The letter went on to refer to some of the difficulties of getting to the area, some hundreds of miles inland, near to the British colony of Rhodesia. [Now the Republic of Zimbabwe.]

'We have found trees right across the road, and have had to cut a way through or round them; we have been stuck for hours in the dry, sandy bed of streams. Up to where our mud hut is we had to cut a road through the bush.'

And as they were living in a tent all this time, with the weather getting hotter and hotter, 'it was with a feeling of great relief and thankfulness that we entered, on October 15th, into possession of our hut at Chiuangumabvu, with the Mission authorised to work, and the site approved by the Governor of the Province'.

It was the end of the first phase of establishing a post for the proclamation of the Gospel in that vast area. It had been a lengthy process. The physical difficulties had

been only part of the obstacles to be overcome, for in
addition political boundaries had stood in the way. The
Portuguese Government had not liked the idea of
having a South African Protestant Mission in their
colonial territory. Understandably, it offended their
national pride. A way round this hindrance had
eventually been found with the help of two Portuguese
Protestants in Lisbon, and a subsidiary branch of the
S.A.G.M. was formed entitled *Missao Evangelica Na
Africa Portuguesa* (Evangelical Mission in Portuguese
Africa). Not until this had taken place could a site be
designated for the establishment of a Mission centre,
and even then the permission of the Governor of the
Province had been required. It had all taken many
negotiations, backed by ardent and persevering prayer,
but in the meantime Gordon and John had been taking
their training at the Colony, and the conviction had
been deepening that Portuguese East Africa was the
place to which they should go.

A few months after the publication of Arthur Brown's
letter an announcement appeared in the S.A.G.M.
magazine to the effect that the first two young men
needed for work in that country had been accepted by
the Mission. Their pictures were given prominence at
the top of the centre page and their names were John E.
Stafford and H. Gordon Legg.

If they had been going to a British Colony like
Rhodesia, or a British Protectorate like Nyasaland,
there would have been nothing to stop them proceeding
there immediately their two years in the Missionary
Training Colony had been completed. Where Portuguese, not English, was the official language, it was
different. They must first learn Portuguese, so to
Portugal the two of them went, each living in the home
of a Portuguese family, where nothing but that language
was spoken. In addition to receiving private tuition they
met each day at school – a primary school where they sat

at the back of the class to learn what they could, along with the children, whose progress often seemed quicker than their own. And there were some things they learned the hard way, as when they set off to the market to buy three kilos of cherries, and were embarrassed to realise, when payment was demanded, that they had evidently asked for thirteen kilos instead.

After some months at school, having obtained some proficiency in the language, they attended classes in the Coimbra University, reputed to be the oldest university in Europe. Here they gained an understanding of Portuguese history and geography, national culture and political aspirations generally. Correct Portuguese manners, too – when to accept and when to refuse an invitation, how to approach officials, where to stand or sit at a reception, the respectful way to addess people in different walks of life . . .

And they observed certain things which put them on their guard, preparing them for what they might encounter under a Portuguese regime in Africa. The power of the priests in a Roman Catholic society – and the power of money, too. They saw how quickly people with several bulging suitcases got through the Customs without even opening them. When their hands went quickly to their pockets, and some coins were surreptitiously passed over, they were waved on by smiling officials while others, with nothing to declare, were required to have their baggage thoroughly investigated. They noted with surprise how some of the dullest children seemed to pass exams, until it dawned on them that their parents had given generous gifts to the appropriate examiners.

'There will be the temptation to take the easy way and get things done more quickly by oiling the wheels with a little bribe', they agreed. It would be something they would have to take a stand against, right from the start, in order to maintain their own integrity. And they

would have to learn how to give due respect to the
government of a Roman Catholic country without
compromising their own evangelical faith. Language
was not the only thing they went to Portugal to learn.
And even when they had completed their ten months'
training in that country, there was still a long and
roundabout journey to be traversed before arriving at
their destination at Chiuangumabvu.

First they had to go to South Africa. For John Stafford
this was home, so he went straight back, but Gordon
returned to England for a round of farewell meetings
before boarding a ship bound for Cape Town. Two
weeks later he was leaning over the side, surveying with
awe the massive range of Table Mountain looming over
the city itself – the city where the Mission to which he
now belonged had been conceived. That was fifty years
ago, when a group of people had been stirred, first by the
appalling conditions in the military camps in South
Africa, then by the needs of the Africans and coloured
people in the ports and mines. In March 1889, they had
formed what was then called the Cape General Mission,
but with the introduction of work in Zululand it
became, in 1894, South Africa General Mission, with
Dr. Andrew Murray as its first president.

Then had followed two or three decades of advance
into the neighbouring countries of Northern and
Southern Rhodesia and Nyasaland. Now, in 1939, the
number of missionaries had increased to nearly three
hundred, drawn not only from South Africa and Great
Britain, but from the U.S.A., Canada and Australia.
The threat of war in Europe was probably already
casting ominous shadows over the administration. But
for Gordon Legg, leaning over the railings to wave back
to John Stafford, there at the quayside to meet him, the
future held no fears. He was young and strong; he and
John were looking forward to working together, and the
sooner they could get on with it, the better.

Getting on with it was not all that easy, as the administration pointed out. Visas to enter Portuguese East Africa in order to engage in Protestant missionary work were not obtained simply on application. The process could take months. Meanwhile, the two young missionary recruits could go to Johannesburg to speak at some meetings there, then go on to stay with Gordon's aunt, Miss Mary Peake Brown, in Swaziland. So to Johannesburg they went, by train, and then on to Swaziland, by train and by bus.

This was their first experience of travelling in a bus full of Africans. Africans with their baskets and their bundles, their live chickens and their dead fish, their bedding and their vegetables. The roads were thick with red dust, and soon the two young white men were covered with a thin coating of it. Fleas jumped over everything, and when John noticed Gordon wriggling uncomfortably and inserting a finger to scratch inside his shirt he murmured with a wry grin, 'Fleas or lice? Now we know why we were warned always to carry insect powder!' The journey seemed interminable, but eventually the bus drew up in a large clearing crowded with men wearing nothing but loin-cloths, and women nothing but skirts. Among them he saw his aunt Mary, neat and smiling in blouse and skirt, with a *terai* (broadbrimmed hat) to shield her head from the sun. Twelve years had passed since he had carried that large parcel to the Post Office, addressed to her. Now he was to see her in her own surroundings, and get his first sight of a mission station in the African bush. This, he found, consisted of three mud huts with thatched roofs in a well swept courtyard with a few trees and a little vegetable garden. Aunt Mary lived in one of the huts, slept in another, and held her clinic in the third. Camp-beds, folding tables and chairs comprised most of the furniture, with boxes and trunks doing duty for cupboards and chests of drawers.

'The floors are smeared with cow dung to keep the fleas low', she explained. 'It dries quickly, and you get used to the smell after a time. Fleas don't like it – they like hopping around in the dust.' When it came to the choice between fleas and dried cow dung, she preferred dried cow dung. What with one thing and another, she didn't know what they would do without cattle. They not only provided edge to edge carpeting in the house, but they pulled bullock carts, produced milk to drink and meat to eat, and their hides provided skirts for the women.

The skirts, she had to admit, were very smelly. 'You'll probably notice it specially on Sunday, when the women are crowded together in church', she warned them.

They *did* notice it...

But they noticed something else, too. After the Sunday service was over, with its enthusiastic singing and children running around unrestrained, its fervent 'Hallelujah's' and its occasional asides as neighbours had a little chat while the sermon was in progress, Aunt Mary came to Gordon and tipped a handful of coins into his hand.

'What's this?' he asked, mystified. It was a little gift from the Christians, she told him. They knew he was her nephew, that he, like her, had come to Africa to preach the good news of forgiveness of sins through faith in Jesus Christ, so they welcomed him, and showed their affection in a practical manner. To them it seemed quite a natural thing to do.

It would have been difficult for him to define his emotions as he looked down at that little pile of coins. These African Christians – they were so poor in earthly possessions, their manner of life was so primitive, their educational opportunities practically nil, yet far from trying to get something from him, they had wanted to give him something. Their broad smiles and hearty greetings were no facade, but genuine, and this spontaneous generosity was the evidence of it. They gave quite willingly. They obviously hadn't stopped to consider whether they might need the money more than he, whether in fact they could afford it. Neither consideration was of importance.

It was the first gift he received from Africans, but it was not the last, not by a long, long way. Again and again, in the years that lay ahead, he was to be moved, almost to tears, by their generosity, by gifts given to him with the open-handedness of warm-hearted brothers.

Aunt Mary was evidently on good terms with royalty, for she took them on one occasion to visit the Swazi Queen Mother, who received them in a hut built the shape of a bee-hive, with an entrance so low they had to bend almost double to enter it. The old lady graciously accepted the mirror they took as a present, and chatted for a while, Aunt Mary interpreting. But when the time came for them to depart they were a bit baffled as to how to make their exit through that awkward aperture. It seemed disrepectful to turn their posteriors on royalty, so they ended by retreating backwards, on hands and knees. But it wasn't the right thing to do, Aunt Mary told them, since 'only dead men come out feet first'.

They stayed with her for a month, and during that time she gave Gordon a piece of advice that he never forgot.

'The time may come when you'll be dissatisfied with the mission leadership', she said, talking frankly. This sort of thing did happen. 'If it happens with you, sit down and write out your complaint fully. Then sleep on it. Then read it again...' She saw her nephew was listening attentively, and concluded with the suspicion of a twinkle in her eye. 'Then tear it up and forget all about it.'

Meanwhile, application had been made for visas for the two young missionaries to reside in Portuguese East

Africa, and no favourable response had been received. 'It's because of the Cardinal', they were told. 'He's very opposed to Protestant Missions, and the Governor is influenced by him. A number of applications by other missionaries have been refused. If the Cardinal says "No!" it is "No!"'

It was decided they should go to Maputo, the capital, to apply in person. The journey was made by coach and train, and they found themselves back in the same sort of environment when they reached Maputo, as they had known in Portugal. There were the same colonnades and balconies, ornamental, colourful buildings and mosaic pavements, the same shrines and rosaries, incense and incantations, the same type of magnificent cathedral. They stayed in a Portuguese guest-house while making periodical visits to government offices, threading their way between the pedestrians and bicycles that thronged the streets and markets. There was very little motorised traffic, beyond the occasional coach. When they had filled in all the forms and answered all the questions put to them, they left the country to await the outcome. This journey involved travelling many more miles, back across the border, and still there was the uncertainty as to whether or not they would be granted their visas.

But it was during this time of constant travel and change of scene that Gordon received the assurance from what he deemed a Higher Authority, that they would obtain what they needed. He was reading in the book of Genesis one day, and came to the end of the twenty-second verse of Chapter twenty-six, and stopped there. He had read the words many times before, but on this occasion they took on a relevant application as though addressed to him personally:

For now the Lord has made room for us, and we shall be fruitful in the land.

That settled it, as far as he was concerned. They were going to live in Portuguese East Africa. The Lord had told him so.

He and John were in Nyasaland when the news came that their visas had been granted. Some time later they learned what had happened. The Cardinal had left Portuguese East Africa for just three months, probably to go to Rome. It was during that period their visas had been cleared.

3

Enemy Territory

To an area twice the size of Wales, lying between the
borders of Southern Rhodesia and Nyasaland [now
Zimbabwe and Malawi], Arthur Brown and his wife
had gone prospecting for a suitable place in which to
establish the first Protestant Mission in that remote part
of Portuguese East Africa. They had travelled in their
Ford lorry over hundreds of miles of dusty inland roads,
passing through scattered villages and vast tracts of
forest and bush country, but nowhere had they found
anything as suitable as Chiuangumabvu on the banks of
the river Luenha, a tributary of the Zambeze river. It
was healthily situated nine hundred feet above sea-level,
there was a reliable water supply, the soil was good, and
within a radius of fifty miles there lived thousands of
tribal people whose language was similar to that spoken
in the part of Nyasaland where they had spent four or
five years.

So at Chiuangumabvu they had settled and Arthur
Brown, slow of speech, but with the pen of a ready
writer, kept careful records of their experiences. He was
an observant man, and very soon after their arrival he
began to be aware of an uncanny undercurrent
dominating the lives of the tribal people among whom
they had settled.

'When we went to Siakulima to preach the Gospel

yesterday afternoon, we heard the strange story that no one was going to plant his garden this season', he wrote in his diary on Monday 23rd November 1936. 'Today, from the workboys, we heard the same story, No one was preparing to plant, or if they had started they had now stopped, and this all over the country. Why? God says they are not to plant. Who said God says so?

'Everybody says so. They had good crops last year. There won't be much rain this year. So God has told them not to plant.'

But as time went on he realised that it was King Lion who had said so. King Lion. Who was King Lion? He heard King Lion referred to from time to time, and as he became more proficient in the language he learned what the people believed, and how deep that faith was in it.

It was a faith linked to a sinister association with the dead of their own clan. It held them to the areas where their families had lived for generations, however dry and barren that land might be. Even in times of drought it held them. Move away to the hills where the water supply could be relied upon? The suggestion was not to be considered for a moment. 'We couldn't do that – our fathers are buried here.' The clan was one, living or dead, and the dead could still exercise control. It was they who could intercede with the rain spirit for the life-giving gift of water. But those dead ancestors had to be propitiated, offerings made to them to persuade them to send rain. Maize, bananas, sweet potatoes; or beer and mush; sometimes sacrifices of goats or fish. Then, if the rain came, the people were reassured not only because of the rain, but because the dead were reconciled to them. And between the living and the dead was the medium, the witch-doctor, of whom the most important was King Lion.

'The people here have long believed that when a big chief dies his spirit enters into a lion and then seeks a medium from among the living by whom the essential communion of the whole clan, living and dead, may be maintained', wrote Arthur Brown. 'This medium is known as "Mambo Mpondolo" – King Lion. There are several of these men, and women, in the land, each one a sort of priest of the spirit of a past great chief now resident in a living lion, and each directly concerned with the making of rain, with thunder and lightning, and with the rainbow.'

These mediums, it appeared, lived quite normal lives most of the time. They married, had children, and were in no way to be distinguished from others until their services were required to propitiate the spirits, or solve some problem demanding extra-sensory powers. How they obtained their positions remained a mystery to Arthur Brown until one day, hearing the lilting of pipes and the chanting of a crowd of people in the distance, he asked one of his workmen, Taundi, about it.

'It's a procession of Kampiao, the King Lion', was the answer. Then Taundi went on to enlarge on the subject. He had known Kampiao when they were both young men living in the same village, he said, adding that he had been present when Kampiao was called to be King Lion. It had happened one evening when little groups of people were sitting, as was their custom, around fires they had kindled, chatting together at the end of the day. The women were at one fire, the men at another, the young unmarried girls at another, and the unmarried men and boys at another. Everything was just as usual, but the conversation round the young men's fire had turned on the matter of the medium for the old chief, Siakulima, who had died some time ago. Who would he be, the new King Lion?

They were talking together in the Nyungwe language, common among the tribes in the area, when suddenly a voice was heard, speaking in the old Tonga speech of their ancestors.

'Kampiao!' the voice called. 'Kampiao! I have

chosen you to be King Lion.'

Kampiao looked up, startled, and said, 'I don't want to be King Lion!'

'Then I will beat you', said the voice. Nothing was seen, but Kampiao was lifted off his feet and flung to the ground, his arms upraised as though to shield himself from blows battering on him. The frightened group of young men scattered, leaving him there, but later they crept back and saw that there were bruises on him. Then they all went off, very subdued, to their sleeping huts.

The following night, sitting round their fire, the mysterious voice was heard again.

'Kampiao, I have chosen you to be King Lion.' This time Kampiao did not resist. 'Yes', he said.

'Then follow me', said the voice, and springing to his feet Kampiao turned, ran into the bush and disappeared. For three days nothing was seen of him, then he returned to the village. He had been with the spirit of Siakulima, he said, and he was therefore now King Lion.

His claim was not accepted outright, although the evidence was in his favour. There were ritual tests to be passed, and the relatives of the old chief were called in from all the villages around to witness them.

The first test involved Kampiao's ability to resist the law of gravity. Two long, unbroken straws of grass were taken from the thatch of the hut of the old chief, and laid on the round. Kampiao laid himself across them. Then four men each took an end of the straws, grasped them with their fingers – and lifted the body of Kampiao into the air. The straws did not break. A gasp went up from the watching crowd – there was Kampiao, suspended as it were in mid-air, on two straws! As the straws were lowered again, his body came slowly down. He had passed the first test – now for the second.

This was a test by fire. A huge pile of dry firewood was lighted, and as the flames leapt up Kampiao walked right into the middle of them and stood there. He remained in the midst of the fire, blowing and spitting, until the flames died down and went out. He stepped out of the embers triumphantly. He was unharmed.

'So we all knew Kampiao was King Lion. Everybody was very happy. We danced and laughed, for King Lion is the rainmaker. When he says there will be rain, there iş rain'.

Arthur Brown was silent for a few moments, his eyes fixed on Taundi's face. The story had been told so vividly, with such detail, it was difficult to doubt it. And yet...

'You are just telling me a yarn, Taundi', he said unbelievingly.

But Taundi was adamant. 'No, Bwana, it is all true. I was there. I saw it with my own eyes', he asserted.

Arthur Brown knew his Bible well. His mind was steeped in it, and while it confirmed him in his confidence that his God was almighty, it left him in no doubt as to the reality of evil spirits. He knew the magicians of Egypt had the power to perform a few, though not all, of the same miracles as Moses. They had turned water into blood, and their rods had become snakes. He knew the dark record of King Saul's visit to the witch of Endor, and how she had brought up one from the realms of death who could foretell the disastrous outcome of the battle on the following day. He knew of Simon the sorcerer, who had successfully bewitched the people of Samaria before Philip the evangelist arrived on the scene. And he had sometimes pondered over such words in the book of Revelation as: 'I know... where thou dwellest, even where Satan's seat is...' [2:13]; and 'he doeth great wonders, so that he maketh fire come down from heaven on the earth in the sight of men, and deceiveth them that dwell on the earth...' [Revelation 13:13,14] If evil powers were limited, it did not mean they did not exist, although he admitted he knew little enough about them, and Taundi's story about Kampiao, the King Lion, puzzled him. It challenged him, too, when he observed that the prediction of drought he had heard about when in Siakulima village in 1936 was fulfilled in 1937. And when, two years later, it was said there would be much rain, and so it proved, he asked himself what was the power behind King Lion, this ordinary African villager who had been called by that mysterious voice into the priesthood of the dead?

He had no doubt that it was to be resisted: '. . . one that maketh his son or his daughter to pass through the fire, or that useth divination, or an observer of times, or an enchanter, or a witch, or a charmer, or a consulter with familiar spirits, or a wizard, or a necromancer. For all that do these things are an abomination unto the Lord' [Deuteronomy 18:10–12]. What concerned him personally was how he would react if he found himself confronted with a human being obviously under the control of an evil spirit. Would he have the courage and the faith to challenge it in the Name of the Lord?

About this time he received a letter from England. It was from a friend of his who had just returned, somewhat perplexed, from a conference of ministers, which he had attended as a delegate. 'The majority there had abandoned belief in a personal devil and demons', he wrote. 'They regarded the attitude of Jesus, as we read it in the New Testament, as an accommodation to an antiquated philosophy no longer acceptable to the modern mind in the light of present day psychology. You are in Africa, where things are reputed to happen. What do you think of it?'

He was soon to be in a position where he could pronounce very definitely what he thought about it. But by that time he and his wife had been joined by two young workers, Gordon Legg and John Stafford, so they were all in it together.

*   *   *

The villagers were frightened. A miasma of fear seemed to have settled on both sides of the river to the north-west of Chiuangumabvu, and all because of one man, Joaquim, King Lion of that district. He was well known in the bush community, had been King Lion for years, but now something alarming had happened to him, enough to scare anyone.

'Chizimu, the great evil spirit, has got him', Arthur was told. 'He's different now. He's mad!' His eyes were wild, he wore nothing but a filthy rag of a loin cloth, seemed to be driven from place to place by some force within, and his behaviour was so fearsome everyone was afraid of what he would do if he met them.

'He sounds like the man of the Gadarenes, out of whom Jesus cast a legion of demons', the four missionaries agreed, as they discussed the matter during their times of prayer and Bible study together. They were challenged by it. It was one thing to read about it in the Bible, affirm faith in Christ's power, believe that the disciples were also empowered, in the Name of Jesus, to cast demons out of people in whom they had made their habitation – but it was another thing to act on it themselves.

'We wondered, if Joaquim should appear again, and it should be possible to talk to him, whether we dare challenge the evil spirit in the Name of the Lord Jesus, and in that Name command it to go. Several times we asked for guidance, and for understanding of God's ways in this warfare', Arthur wrote later, adding honestly: 'Then, with the non-appearance of Joaquim and the pressure of other things, we forgot about him, and our prayers.'

So he was quite unprepared for the confrontation when it came. He was on his back under the Ford lorry, as it happened, trying to find out what was wrong with the engine, when he became aware of someone standing watching him, and twisting his head, looked up and saw it was Joaquim.

He knew intuitively that the moment had come, and with a wordless but urgent prayer for God's empowering scrambled to his feet and started talking.

'How are you, Joaquim?' he asked kindly, wondering if he would be rebuffed. The last time Joaquim had appeared in the neighbourhood he had been muttering and talking all the time, dribbling onto his straggly beard, wild-eyed and angry, until he had eventually run off, cursing. But now the man stood wearily, his gaunt frame drooping, and he answered dully:

'Ill. The spirit drives me everywhere. I'm so tired, but it drives me on and on.'

'Where are you going now?'

'Down river. To walk and walk and walk. Ill, but it drives me on...'

'Joaquim,' said Arthur quietly but steadily. 'Do you want to be delivered from this evil spirit?'

'Yes, I do,' was the reply. 'I'm so tired.' He held out his skinny arms and looked at them. 'So tired and so thin...'

Then Arthur told him about Jesus. Jesus, Lord of all spirits, the Saviour who had come to suffer and die for the sins of mankind, who had risen from the dead, mighty conqueror of death and demons. The one who could free Joaquim here and now from the evil power that was driving him to his death.

It was all very quiet and unemotional. After he had explained who Jesus was and what He had done, Arthur prayed, then suggested Joaquim should ask this King Jesus to deliver him. There was silence for what seemed a long time, then Arthur put his arm gently round Joaquim's shoulder saying, 'The King Jesus wants you. Give yourself to Him.'

That seemed to unloose what was bottled up, for Joaquim, without any further encouragement, started to come out with all his sins, going into some detail over them, then his possession by evil spirits – and his weariness, his exhaustion. At the end he said simply:

'If this that I have heard of You is true, save me, Jesus.'

Suddenly Arthur was conscious of a moving in his own spirit, such as he had never known before, and looking into Joaquim's eyes said:

'Evil spirits, whoever you are, in the Name of the Lord Jesus Christ, go out of that man!' He did not know what to expect, but everything remained very quiet, except for the usual incessant buzzing of flies and droning of insects, and a minute or two passed before Joaquim stirred. Then he said, in a matter of fact voice,

'I'm not going down river. I'm going to stay here.'

'So you shall,' said Arthur reassuringly; and the two of them walked slowly down the hill, back to the cluster of huts and people passing to and fro among them, who looked with amazement at the missionary and the emaciated Joaquim quietly walking beside him. Briefly Arthur explained what had happened, that the Lord Jesus was greater in power than King Lion or Chizimu, and now Joaquim needed something to eat, and somewhere to sleep.

The following morning Joaquim, fitted out with an old pair of shorts and a shirt, was sent off with an axe to cut firewood. 'Better to keep him occupied', the missionaries agreed. The rising drum had already sounded, the workmen engaged in building had gathered for the short service when Arthur read some of the few portions of Scripture he had been able to translate into their language, then after prayer they had all dispersed to their various tasks. Arthur's job each morning was to help Gordon and John with language study, but he cut it rather short on this occasion. His mind was on Joaquim, and after a couple of hours he set off to see how he was getting on.

He found him, a few logs beside him, looking intently

down the valley.

'Bwana,' he said, 'that spirit has been worrying me. He said he wanted to come into me again. He begged me to let him in. He said he was wandering about in the desert places, without anywhere to rest.'

Arthur gave a little start. What Joaquim was saying was almost exactly what he had read many times in the Gospel according to Luke, the words of the Lord Jesus Christ Himself:

'When the unclean spirit is gone out of a man, he walketh through dry places seeking rest; and finding none, he saith, I will return unto my house whence I came out.'

So that is what actually happened in the unseen realm of which he was suddenly being made so acutely aware through Joaquim! And although Arthur could see no spirit, Joaquim evidently could, for he pointed down the valley saying, 'He's gone off down there. He was cursing me, and everyone who believed in Jesus, and told me to leave this place. When I said I wouldn't, because I was at peace here, he cursed me again, and I began to be afraid. Then you came, and he's gone off...'

But the spirit returned, again and again, when Joaquim was alone, sometimes wheedling, sometimes threatening, but always with the same request. He wanted to re-enter Joaquim, and it was wearing Joaquim down. Neither Arthur and his wife, nor Gordon and John could understand why, in spite of their continued and earnest prayers, the deliverance was not complete. Then, one day, a thought came to mind which shed light on the problem. Was Joaquim holding on to something that gave the spirit a foothold? 'Neither give place to the devil.' Was there an area which had not been completely yielded to the control of the Holy Spirit? As soon as Arthur had the opportunity he broached the subject to Joaquim.

'Have you still got anything belonging to King Lion

in your possession?' he asked. There was silence for a moment or two, then Joaquim answered rather reluctantly, 'Yes – I've got a few medicines and a cloth.' Then he added wistfully, 'It's the best cloth I've got'. He was a poor man, and that length of cloth was very valuable to him, because of its quality. Perhaps, also, it gave him a certain status in the clan, as its owner. He did not want to part with it, but when Arthur told him that as long as he had anything associated with King Lion the evil spirit would have a hold over him, he evidently saw the point. What inner struggles he had over relinquishing that length of cloth and the few medicines, the missionaries never knew. They said nothing more about it to him, for the decision must be his own. All they could do was to pray for him. But at the next afternoon class meeting, held in the open air and attended by a number of the local tribespeople who were turning to the living God, he got up and announced that he had thrown away everything connected with King Lion. He did not want them any more. 'For now I have a Saviour.'

Never again did the spirit pester Joaquim as before, though he heard it again, this time not near to him, but on the roof of the missionaries' house. He told Arthur about it.

'Bwana,' he said. 'I want to tell you something. You ought to know that every night a spirit comes on the roof of your house and curses you. It curses you all for coming to this country. It curses you for speaking of Jesus Christ. He hates to hear the people here praying to Jesus. He hates you and curses you, that you may die, or be driven away.'

'We are not afraid of him,' replied Arthur. 'Our Lord Jesus is mightier than the spirits, all of them.'

Although the spirit ceased to trouble Joaquim as before, pressure was brought to bear on him from another source. His relatives arrived at the mission station from a number of villages, very upset that he was settling there. They argued with him and pleaded with him to return to his own village, to the land of his ancestors, and to their worship. He was offending the spirits, they said, and the spirits would take their revenge.

But Joaquim was adamant. He had found peace in this place, and in trusting the Lord Jesus, and he refused to go back. The change in him was so evident that his wife was persuaded to come across the river with their children and join him. This was the final break with the old tradition, and the power of the pull of the dead was broken. Even when one of their children became seriously ill, they did not waver, nor yield to the urgent persuasion of their relatives who said, 'We told you so! The curse is upon you. You have offended the spirits. Come back, offer the sacrifices they demand, or your child will die.'

But in answer to prayer in the Name of Jesus, the child lived.

The spirit made one more effort to seduce Joaquim, who told Arthur about it.

'The spirit has been here again, Bwana,' he said. 'He told me I need not be afraid to do what they tell me because, he said, "We believe in God, too".'

Arthur was amazed – and indignant. The craftiness of it! Joaquim had no Bible to turn to, he had never read the words of the apostle John, warning the uninstructed against the very subtlety the spirit was using. Arthur put the translation of the Scriptures into the tribal language high on his priorities. He spent most of his time on it, and incidents like this confirmed him in his decision to do so.

'Listen!' he said emphatically to Joaquim. 'That spirit is a deceiving spirit. Don't listen to it. The evil spirits' belief in God is different from yours. They are His enemies. The Book of God says, 'the devils also believe – *and tremble*!' They know God is, and they are in terror of Him. The Book of God says: "Resist the devil, and he will flee from you". It also says "Draw near to God, and he will draw near to you". Let us pray to Him now, Joaquim, that He may shelter us from this evil enemy.'

          *   *   *

'We're in spiritual warfare here,' said Arthur solemnly, later on, as he related this last effort of the spirit to draw Joaquim away. Gordon and John sat silent, listening to him, aware of the reality of unseen evil powers in a way they had never known in their own countries. They were entering Satan's territory, where his power had been unchallenged until now. 'We need to take to ourselves the whole armour of God, if we are to withstand in the evil day – and go on standing!'

4

King Lion

The year 1939 was a significant one in the annals of the
S.A.G.M., as well as in the history of Gordon Legg and
John Stafford. While the two young men were starting
their missionary careers in the west of Portuguese East
Africa, negotiations were going on in the eastern
province of Zambezia which were to have a direct
bearing on their lives in years to come.

It was here, in the port of Quelimane, that Vasco da
Gama, the intrepid Portuguese explorer, landed in 1498
on his voyage of discovery to find a sea route from
Europe to India. The subsequent conquest of the whole
vast area by the Portuguese was accompanied by the
arrival of Roman Catholic priests, who built churches
and cathedrals, and propagated their faith over wide
areas. The whole of the north of the country was without
any Protestant witness until 1913 when the Presbyterian
Church of Scotland established a mission centre at
Mihecani, near the administrative post of Nauela, some
two hundred and fifty miles inland from Quelimane.
Twenty years later, in 1933, the entire responsibility
and authority for the work started by the Presbyterians
was handed over to the Nyasa Mission, centred in
Nyasaland. But the Nyasa Mission lacked the personnel
and finance to develop it, and in 1939, turning to the
S.A.G.M. for help, passed it over to that society,

handing on complete control. It was a well grounded
work, with a Primary School attended by 400 children,
a health centre with dispensary and maternity department, and the church itself was well established, with
elders already appointed, and a number of outstations
opened, but needing frequent visitation. Such an
opportunity could not be ignored. The area around
Mihecani was far more thickly populated than at
Chiuangumabvu, and the people more civilised, but
equally ignorant of the way of salvation through faith in
Christ alone. The Browns, in remote Chiuangumabvu,
with their experience and knowledge of the language,
were asked to move to Mihecani, leaving Gordon and
John, two years after their arrival there, alone in the
pioneering area.

By this time they had become accustomed to the
manner of life of the tribal people near whom they lived;
they employed a few of them to work on their own land
to engage in building projects, plant vegetables, carry
water and firewood, fish and hunt for food, grind grain,
and generally provide the necessities that could not be
bought in any other way in such primitive surroundings.
Their own time was taken up with visiting villages far
and wide, to preach and teach, and also to continue the
translation of the Bible into the local language. This had
been started some forty years earlier, by a Roman
Catholic priest from Italy, so there was something to
build on. And Arthur Brown had translated some
hymns and choruses, the first of which was:

> Jesus loves me, this I know,
> For the Bible tells me so.
> Little ones to Him belong
> They are weak, but He is strong.
>   Yes, Jesus loves me...

But the chorus that perhaps meant most to them in those

days was another that Arthur Brown had translated, and which they sometimes sang almost as though raising it like a shield against the enemy:

> There is power, power, wonder-working power,
> In the blood of the Lamb
> There is power, power, wonder-working power,
> In the precious blood of the Lamb.

For, as Gordon wrote many years afterwards:

> At that time we were specially conscious of the powers of darkness, and the spiritual hosts of wickedness in the heavenly places, and the efficacy of the precious blood of Christ to protect us.

They were constantly encountering evidences of the superstitions of the tribespeople. They knew why a broken earthenware pot was to be seen at a place where two paths met. The ashes under it and the feathers of a chicken told their own story. A sacrifice had been made to appease the Great Spirit. They knew what was going on when from time to time they heard the sounds of drunken revelry coming from a nearby village. A goat had been drowned in beer, to appease the Great Spirit, and now the beer was making its way down thirsty throats. And they knew why, when a lion was killed, there was such an urgent desire to obtain and eat its heart. Whoever did so would, it was believed, after death be raised a lion, king of the forest.

Gordon and John were never quite clear what it was thought happened if a lion killed was one of the tribe's ancestors.

The superstitions connected with lions were somewhat confusing, but they were not sufficiently binding to prohibit the slaughter of a man-eater when possible. Having only spears, bows and arrows, it was not an easy task, and on one occasion Gordon was persuaded to try his hand at shooting one. A 303 rifle had been left in his possession by a Portuguese friend in the locality who had gone back to Portugal on holiday, and Gordon, knowing how many people had been killed by man-eaters (49 in one year), decided it was his duty to have a go at lion hunting. The small kid of a goat was tied to a tree in an open space in the garden, as an enticement, and sure enough, just about sunrise, a crouching lion was seen approaching. Gordon fired, and to his own amazement the lion rolled over in the sand. He had hit it! But it wasn't dead yet. It dragged itself away, and warning cries from the Africans hidden in the bush, and from John, who was preparing breakfast and appeared on the verandah when he heard the shot, were unanimous.

'Don't go after it! It's dangerous! Stay where you are!' A lion wounded could be as ferocious as one robbed of its whelps. It was not until some time later, after a blazing fire had driven the lion into the water and it had crawled out again in a clearing that Gordon, by this time up a tree, fired the fatal shot and killed it. It took eight men to carry it up to the house, where it was skinned, and found to measure nine feet, eight inches from head to tail. Great was the rejoicing, with spears triumphantly upraised, that another man-eater had been slain.

But in spite of strict instructions that no part of the carcase was to be removed, Gordon and John later discovered that though it still appeared to be intact, the heart had been removed ...

They were not again personally involved with lions, though they might well have been, for the only protection they had in their windows was wire-netting to keep the mosquitoes out. One thrust of a lion's paw would have ripped it, and there were mornings when spoor on the verandah told of visits from the king of the forest during the night. But angels are just as real as evil spirits in the unseen realm, and invested with a superior authority – so perhaps that is why no lions entered the flimsily protected dwelling, and why even the herds of elephants that sometimes went through the carefully planted gardens kept to the footpaths!

However, although Gordon and John generally avoided encounters with wild beasts, they were very much involved in the lives of the scattered tribal community. Often they were called on to help solve questions relating to the Portuguese authorities or to administer first-aid to cuts and fractured limbs, and dispense medicine for various ills. Their little cupboard contained supplies of aspirin, castor oil, Epsom salts, quinine, and other simple remedies which, backed by their own fervent prayers, seemed to work wonders. But sometimes they found themselves drawn into affairs and experiences which they were at a loss to explain, and this was especially so in the case of the poisoned children.

It all started for them one night when they had retired to bed early, hoping to sleep soundly for the first time for some weeks. The rains had come at last, bringing a measure of coolness to the humid, stifling atmosphere, and since no one wanted to be out in the rain unnecessarily, they were unlikely to have visitors on a wet night. The sound of a cough outside on the verandah awakened them – a cough was the local equivalent to knocking on the front door. They both emerged from their rooms hurriedly, for the cough was urgent and agitated. Standing there in the pouring rain was Ncebola, one of their workmen, and almost before Gordon had time to ask what was the matter the man blurted out:

'Bwana, come quickly! The children of Nkuskansawawa are dying! They are screaming with pain. Please come and heal them!'

'Nkuskansawawa's children! All right! We'll come immediately!' Dragging on their trousers and shirts,

they snatched a few medicines from their little
dispensary and set off with Ncebola along the muddy
paths, slipping and sliding as they went, the tall grasses
through which they passed showering them with
raindrops. On the way they gleaned what they could
from Ncebola.

'Those children – they're vomiting so violently, and
screaming. All except little Tembo. He's dead already.'

'Tembo – dead!' The little five-year-old was the
youngest of the three children, all of whom they knew.
They quickened their steps.

'It looks as though they've been poisoned', said
Ncebola. Poisoned!

The oil lamp they held aloft cast weird shadows across
the path that was familiar enough in the daytime, and
which they knew was only two miles long, but it seemed
strange and endless now. But at last they reached the
clearing where eight huts and a goat-house and a barn
comprised the part of the village they were making for,
and entering Nkuskansawawa's hut they saw his wife
holding in her arms a boy writhing with pain, while the
older one rolled on a rush mat, groaning.

'Whatever it is, it will have passed through their
stomachs to their intestines by this time,' Gordon and
John murmured to each other. 'Pray God we give them
the right thing.' All they knew of medical treatment was
what they had learned while in the Missionary Training
Colony at the Croydon General Hospital, or picked up
by experience in their own dispensary. 'Castor oil?' The
hut was full of smoke from the embers of the fire, and
their eyes stung as they opened their little medical case,
poured out the doses and administered them to the
children. Then they turned to the parents.

'We will pray to our Lord Jesus, and ask Him to heal
them . . . Let's pray.'

The night wore on, and as they talked together, little
by little the story came out of what had happened.

Nkuskansawawa and his wife had gone off to their maize
garden, some distance away, leaving the three boys,
aged nine, seven and five, to take the goats to the river
for a drink, then into the bush to graze where there was
grass. They had done this many times before. Late in the
afternoon the three children had returned, and to their
delight had seen a dish of mush on the floor just inside
their hut. Without a second thought they had pounced
on it, and in no time at all had gobbled it up.

Then the retching had started. And the vomiting.
When the parents returned they found their children
doubled up with pain, and when little Tembo died
before their eyes, they had urged Ncebola to run to the
missionaries for help.

As they crouched together in the hut, anxiously
watching the two boys who at last lay back, exhausted
but no longer in pain, they whispered one to another:

'They were all well when we left them this
morning... and now, little Tembo – dead!'

'Let's look and see if there's anything left in the dish –
no, nothing. The boys ate it all up.'

'That mush. Who put it there? It must have been
poisoned...'

By the time morning broke the whole village knew
what had happened, and the chief took charge. In a
more civilised area the police would have been called in,
detectives would have been making discreet enquiries,
the forensic experts would have been consulted, people
called in for questioning, the whole mechanism of the
law set in motion. Here in the African bush, it was
different.

'There will be trial by "*Wabve*",' the chief decreed,
and went off to see Kampiao, the King Lion, about it.
Kampiao collected certain roots and leaves, boiled them
in water, and on the day appointed produced the
concoction while the crowd that had gathered looked on
apprehensively. Everyone in the neighbourhood was

there – none was exempt. It was trial by *Wabve*, and all
must be tested to find out who had put the poisoned
mush into Nkuskansawawa's hut.

The chief made a speech first, explaining what they
all knew – that everyone must drink the brew the King
Lion had made. Those who swallowed it, then vomited
it up, were innocent. The one who swallowed and
retained it was guilty.

Kampiao, dressed in all his regalia of leopard skin and
skull cap, charms dangling from his neck, wrists and
ankles, face whitened with powdered tobacco, took
charge. He screamed. He leaped in the air. He went into
contortions, screamed again, and eventually started
speaking gibberish that no one could understand. The
moment had come. The spirit of King Lion had spoken!
The concoction was poured into a gourd, and solemnly
handed from one to another, and as each one swallowed
a mouthful there was a tense silence, then a sort of sigh of
relief as one after another vomited it up.

Then the gourd was handed to Bete. Bete was one of
the older workmen at Chiuangumabvu who had
formerly been employed by the local government
authority to kill locusts. He was sufficiently well-off to
have more than one wife, and they were all with him
now. They watched him take a mouthful of the *Wabve*,
saw him swallow it, and then try to spew it out. But he
could not. He retched and coughed in vain, and a gasp
went up from the waiting crowd as the chief went
forward saying sternly, 'You are the man!'

Then it came out, as Bete confessed to the chief. He
and Nkuskansawawa had been at enmity for years, he
admitted. They had quarrelled, stolen each other's
grain, invoked the aid of the witch-doctor to curse each
other's crops, so that they would not produce.
Sometimes the curse had worked, sometimes it hadn't.
But things had come to a head and Bete, seizing his
opportunity when the hut was empty, had put in the

mush, mixed with the poison he had used to kill the locusts.

The chief and the King Lion had taken the law into their own hands up to this point, but beyond that they dare not go. The Portuguese authorities claimed the right to pass judgment on criminals found guilty of murder and manslaughter, so Bete was escorted to the nearest *Posto*, sixty miles away, and sentenced to a long term of imprisonment with hard labour.

It had happened so quickly that when it was over Gordon and John scarcely knew how to interpret the strangeness of the event. There could be no doubt that the trial by *Wabve* had been effective, that the culprit had been promptly and clearly revealed, and so brought to justice. Had the build-up of the witch-doctor's incantations so preyed on the emotions of the guilty party that when the test came he was psychologically affected and could not vomit, try as he would to do so? Had the spirit of King Lion chosen to reveal the truth in answer to Kampiao's cries and contortions, thus demonstrating its power and superior knowledge? Or was it a case of the Most High God, whose eyes are in every place, beholding the evil and the good, who had overruled, in spite of man's ignorance, to bring about righteous judgment? They knew that a similar test to that of the *Wabve* was decreed in the Levitical law, when a woman whose husband suspected her of adultery, could bring her before the priest, who would give her to drink holy water mixed with dust from the tabernacle floor. If she swelled up, she was guilty. If she did not, she was innocent. Was the trial by *Wabve* in the same category?

They did not know. Some things, they had to admit, were beyond their understanding. What they did know was that people sometimes died when there was no other explanation than that they had been cursed by the witch-doctor, who had been paid to do so. 'We knew by personal experience that we were engaged in a spiritual battle against the powers of darkness,' Gordon wrote many years later, and he learned by personal experience, too, the truth of the words he had often sung, when still in England:

> Precious Blood, by this we conquer,
> In the fiercest fight
> Sin and Satan overcoming
> By its might.

Gordon was thirty-three years old when, in 1946, he went back to England on furlough. Until that time, although he had made visits to the neighbouring countries of Rhodesia, Nyasaland and South Africa, Chiuangumabvu had been his home. It was here that he had learned the African way of life and thought, learned to endure loneliness and privation, learned mysteries of the unseen world. As Arthur Brown said, he could assert with assurance that 'when Jesus spoke of the devils and of demons, He was not making any concessions to an antiquated philosophy held by the Jews, nor will He make any concessions now to modern psychology. He was speaking most sober and solemn truths to which we do well to pay heed all the world over, and not only in Africa.'

He never returned to Chiuangumabvu to live, although he and other missionaries visited the area from time to time to teach and encourage the scattered believers there. There had been changes in the whole social structure, for the Portuguese authorities introduced a system whereby the able-bodied men were recruited to go away and work in factories or on plantations, at a pittance, for several months each year. The area became depopulated as a result, with the women, old people and children eking out their existence as best they could. John Stafford, married by this time, was transferred to Mihecani, and although Gordon was willing to go back to Chiuangumabvu alone, the Mission leaders decided against it. So, after a year in what is now Zimbabwe, he too, went to Mihecani. A new era in his life had begun.

5

Mihecani

Mihecani, 'at the place where the miheca trees grow', derived its name from a grove of miheca trees growing round a large granite rock somewhere near the centre of the province of Zambesia. It was here that the first missionaries had decided to settle, and in order to do so they had first had to get the bush cleared. There they had started the slow process of having huts and houses built to replace the tents with which they had arrived, while they applied themselves to learning the local language, teaching and preaching in it as best they could. This was away back in the early part of the century, and the pioneering period was over by the time Gordon eventually arrived there in 1947.

He found the area in which the Mission was centred a well ordered clearing, with an imposing church, several other brick buildings, a few thatched huts, and a vegetable garden in which were grown a variety of fruits and vegetables to supplement the local diet, which consisted mainly of sweet potatoes, grain and beans. It lay back about a mile from the dusty main road, along which very little wheeled traffic passed, apart from a few bicycles ridden by Africans, and the occasional car belonging to Portuguese managers of nearby plantations or one of the Fathers at the Roman Catholic Mission only a mile away.

John Stafford was in charge of the school. There was
not much to do regarding the allocation of classrooms,
which were practically non-existent. Classes were
mainly held out of doors under the trees, or in the
church. The children all went home during the rainy
season. The appointment of teachers was a greater
responsibility. Among those fifteen or so teachers were
two who were to have dramatic, though vastly different
effects on the Protestant church in the country in years
to come. One of them, Cornelio Muhiua, was well-
educated by local standards, for he had attended a
Portuguese school, and spoke the language fluently.
Martinho Campos, on the other hand, was a rather
diffident young man from a village some miles away,
who had little enough to say for himself, being conscious
that his academic qualifications fell far below those of
some of the other teachers. Both of them attended
church services regularly, taught in the Sunday School,
and visited the outstations. There was little at that time
to indicate how differently they would develop.

The main concern of both Gordon and John during
those early years in Mihecani was how to reach the little
villages that lay scattered thinly over the hundreds of
miles that spread southward to the Zambeze River and
northward to the railroad that ran from Nyasaland to
the coast. Mihecani was the only Evangelical mission
centre in the whole area. Literacy among the Africans
throughout the country was only about eighteen per
cent. Bibles were in short supply, and in any case, only
obtainable in Portuguese. A few portions of Scripture
had been translated into the tribal languages, although
the whole of the New Testament and Psalms was being
made available in Lomwe, the language mainly used in
the Mihecani area. But there were no commentaries, no
Christian books, and no long-term training courses. The
Gospel had been spread almost entirely by word of
mouth, often by people whose own understanding of it

was limited to what they had heard. The marvel was that so many had responded, and that little groups, here and there, had built their own thatched prayer huts in which to sing the hymns and recite the verses they had been taught, and pray together.

Getting round by bicycle or the old Ford lorry to visit these groups was a primary claim on John's and Gordon's time. Their senior missionary, Mr. Proctor, usually conducted the Sunday services in Mihecani. It was the only place where meetings could be depended on to start at the time appointed, with most of the congregation present. Mr. Proctor had achieved the seemingly impossible in this respect, and he had done it by starting punctually, even if the church was empty. It had taken a long time for the tribal people to learn that when the bell tolled it meant that the service would begin in so many minutes, and that if they strolled in an hour or so later, Senhor Proctor would not have waited for them. He would have done what he said, and started the meeting when the bell stopped tolling – and now the singing and the praying and the preaching was all over, and they had missed it! Dismay, incredulity and even remonstrance had failed to make the Senhor relax his inexplicable insistence that ten o'clock meant ten o'clock, and eventually his determination won the day. At Mihecani church members turned up for meetings on time.

It was by no means his only achievement, but it was so unusual and distinctive that it was one by which he was always remembered by his junior workers who gratefully reaped the benefit.

Although the missionaries had known of several Protestant missions in the south of the country, until 1949 they had known of no other Protestant work north of the Zambeze. One day in that year however, some men arrived on bicycles from the two provinces of Niassa and Nampula, north of the railroad, and presented themselves with the earnest plea that someone would come and teach them more about the Bible, and about the Lord Jesus Christ. They had been travelling for four days, and the story they had to tell was apostolic. Here is the gist of it.

Some time in the mid 1930s, an African pastor in neighbouring Nyasaland [now Malawi], had crossed the border from the comparative security of the British Protectorate into the alien atmosphere of the Portuguese colony for one purpose, and one purpose only. Impelled by the command to go into all the world and preach the Gospel to every creature, he had responded to the challenge of the millions of fellow Africans there who knew nothing of salvation through faith in Christ. Visiting the villages and plantations near the railway line he had slowly moved eastward, preaching as he went, and many had believed. He hadn't had an easy time of it – quite the reverse, in fact. The Roman Catholic priests, backed often by local authorities, had opposed him strenuously, and he had known not only threats and court cases, but beatings and imprisonments as well. But like the apostle Paul, none of these things had deflected him from his purpose. Suffering for Christ's sake was something he expected and was prepared for, for had not his Master said that through much tribulation we must enter the Kingdom of Heaven? Faithfully he had crossed the border, year after year, spending several months in Portuguese territory, visiting and encouraging the isolated little groups that were the fruit of his witness, before travelling on to carry his message to regions beyond. In this, as in other respects, Pastor Herman Kajao had set his converts a good example, for they saw what Jesus meant when He spoke about His disciples taking up the cross to follow Him. But now he was old, and his visits less frequent, and his converts were hungry for spiritual food. So when they heard that there were white missionaries in their own country, south of the railroad, who preached the same Gospel as Pastor Kajao, they sent to enquire further.

Their arrival opened up a whole new field for Gordon and John, and permanent links were formed with the scattered believers in the north, eventually resulting in the formation of the Evangelical Church of Nauela. But long before that happened Mihecani had become the acknowledged centre of Protestant activity throughout the whole country north of the Zambeze. Writing home in 1949 Gordon reported:

'Shortly after I arrived the annual conference meetings were held, when at one meeting there were 1,500 Africans, about 600 at the Children's service, and 400 at the Lord's table . . . Many of these had come from the district in the north where there is no European missionary residing but where, through the labours of an African, burdened for souls, there are now more than 1,000 baptised believers meeting in over 100 groups scattered throughout a vast area.'

They came to Mihecani, not only for the Annual Conference, but when they needed help and encouragement.

'Only last week we heard of eight Christians from one of these districts who were imprisoned – the influence of Rome we believe – for they were not willing to attend their services . . . Remember these brethren in their hour of persecution that their faith may not fail, but like Paul and Silas may pray and sing praises and that other prisoners may hear of the Lord.

'The four men who had cycled four days to bring this report pleaded with me to visit them if at all possible this year . . . Pray that if this should be God's will, doors may be opened with necessary permits forthcoming, so making the trip possible. Last time the journey was made by cycle, each person carrying clothing and food for the three weeks trek. I am quite willing to cycle this time . . .' but he admitted that he would be very glad if he could obtain a car for such purposes, as it would make travelling so much quicker, and enable him to travel so many more of the hundreds of miles along the dusty, bumpy roads that separated the various groups.

How to obtain that much-needed motor vehicle was a constantly recurring question in his thoughts those days. He had been encouraged to hope that he could buy one in Quelimane at a reduced price, and he made the three hundred mile journey there with high hopes of returning to Mihecani driving his own car. But the transaction did not materialise, and as he had arranged to visit Chiuangumabvu, he had to go there by bus after all. A brief report in a letter written a few weeks later referred to what he found there.

'It was good to see the desire of some to know more of the way of Life, and to find most going on with the Lord. Although there is no evangelist or missionary, each week eight or ten meet for singing and prayer, and repeating the texts learnt by heart. Only one man is able to read, a polygamist named Melo.' Melo was only an immature Christian, but he would be able to read aloud to the others, and so they would all learn more. And the invisible Lord in whom they trusted was with them. One advantage they had over the Protestants in the more thickly populated areas was that they would encounter no opposition from Roman Catholic priests, for there were none in the neighbourhood.

Gordon was not discouraged, but he was weary as he continued his journey westward. He had planned to cross over the border into Rhodesia [Zimbabwe] and spend a few days at the S.A.G.M. centre in Rusitu before returning to Mihecani. He had spent most of the previous year there, filling in for a missionary who was on furlough, and had enjoyed it. There were none of the restrictions on Protestant missionaries in Rhodesia that hampered the work in Portuguese East Africa, and as

English, not Portuguese, was the official language, life
was easier all round. The eight Rusitu missionaries were
not only responsible for a well established central
church with a large number of outstations to be visited
regularly, but a clinic and a boarding-school as well. It
was a lonely life he had been leading in Mihecani,
especially since John Stafford and his wife had left for
furlough earlier in the year, and going back to Rusitu
was like visiting home. He was not one to reveal his
feelings freely, and in the letter he wrote to his
supporters in Great Britain after that short holiday he
only referred to it very briefly.

'God blessed me during that visit, and He only knows
how I needed a fresh touch from Him', was all that he
disclosed. The rest of the letter contained information
about the progress of the work generally. Only after it
was ended did a postscript, added by his brother, give
the information that on October 6th, 1949, Gordon
hoped to marry Miss K. Allen of the Rusitu mission. So
commenced a relationship which was to strengthen and
enrich his life and his service in the tumultuous years
that lay ahead.

*   *   *

Miss K. Allen, known to her friends and colleagues as
Katie, was a nurse/midwife from Wales, and had been
in charge of the Rusitu clinic for several years when
Gordon asked her to marry him. His diffidence in
making the proposal was because she was obviously very
happy where she was, and filling an important role
there. If she left, the clinic would be without a fully
qualified midwife, and although there were African
aides whom she had trained capable of handling most of
the cases that came in, it would be difficult to find
someone to replace her in the position of responsibility.
However in this respect, Rusitu's loss proved to be
Mihecani's gain, for shortly after the Leggs were

married the Proctors went on furlough, and during that
time the clinic in Mihecani became Katie's responsibility. And as her experience and training had extended
far beyond her midwifery course, she found herself
called on to deal with situations that would normally
have been left to a doctor. But, as they both freely
acknowledged, without prayer Katie's professional
skills would have been inadequate for some of the cases
that came her way. As it was, she gained quite a
reputation, not only as a nurse and midwife, but as one
who could diagnose the condition of patients very
accurately.

Katie was a happy person. She had been happy in
Rusitu, but admitted quite frankly that she was even
happier in Mihecani – with Gordon. There was,
perhaps, another, though different reason for her
satisfaction at being in the Portuguese colony. It went
right back to her days in Bible College when she had
attended a missionary meeting in which the main
speaker was a Mrs. Claridge, who had a most moving
story to tell.

She and her husband, members of the S.A.G.M., had
been working near Blantyre in Nyasaland, under British
rule, where there had been an encouraging response to
the preaching of the Gospel. But they had become
increasingly aware of the spiritual needs of the Africans
in the neighbouring Portuguese colony, and at last had
decided to cross the border, to do what they could to
carry in there the message of salvation through faith in
Christ. It was while they were on one of those
evangelistic tours that Mr. Claridge had contracted
blackwater fever and died. The African carriers who
were with them took fright and fled, leaving the young
widow alone. There in that isolated place she had dug a
grave deep enough to bury her husband's body, piling
stones on top to preserve it from scavenging animals,
before finding her way back to Nyasaland. Still fired

with the same compassion for the African tribes as had urged her husband forward to reach them, she was now pleading for others to take his place. The mental picture of that lonely grave far away in East Africa challenged many hearts in Great Britain during those days of the 1920s. Arthur Brown was one who heard God's call to Portuguese East Africa through it, and his establishing of Chiuangumabvu as the S.A.G.M.'s first mission station there was the direct result. Katie Allen was another, and the fulfilment of a desire born 25 years earlier came when, as Gordon Legg's wife, she set out with him to visit that grave, 130 miles from Mihecani.

There was something very significant to them in the fact that shortly before setting out they had come, in their morning Bible reading together, to the words, 'Except a corn of wheat fall into the ground and die, it abideth alone: but if it die, it bringeth forth much fruit' [John 12:24]. It seemed like a Divine confirmation of the promise of fruit from that life laid down.

They would have been unable to find the place where Mr. Claridge's body had been buried had they not gone to the local administration office, but there they were supplied with a guide who led them for nearly an hour through the bush.

'A heap of stones with a cross on top marks the place where Mrs. Claridge, in her loneliness, laid her husband to rest,' wrote Katie. 'Seeing the desolation and isolation at the foot of the rugged hills made us realise what a price they had paid to bring the Gospel to this land. As we stood there and talked and prayed with the few who had gathered, we were challenged afresh with the tremendous need of the vast area without a testimony to His Name.

'But He Himself said "... if it die, it bringeth forth much fruit". We gave thanks to God for the first signs of life in the meeting together of two or three groups of believers about 100 miles away, but we believe that this

was not the full fruition of that seed which fell into the
ground so many years ago.

'Some consider that missionary work in this part of
Africa is so discouraging, difficult, scope of operations so
limited, doors nearly closing, and labourers so few that it
is not worth while continuing'. But that was not her
view. 'Do you not believe that lives laid down here will,
in the purpose of God, produce an abundant harvest?'
she wrote, adding spiritedly:

'We do!'

6

Priestly Opposition

There at Mihecani it was not always a simple matter to distinguish between active demonic influence and mere superstition. Gordon knew enough about occult powers through his experiences at Chiuangumabvu to convince him of their reality, but he and Katie both knew, too, how those very powers could deceive, and that the people were often gripped by quite needless alarm. The ills and disasters that beset mankind anywhere were often attributed to the secret curse of the witch doctor, and maladies that might have been healed with normal care and hygiene were only intensified by ignorance and fear. When the wife of Martinho Campos gave birth to a boy who was deformed, there were those who murmured that she was under a curse. When her next boy was also deformed, the murmurs increased. Even though she and Martinho did not believe it, it was hard for them to assert their confidence in an all-powerful God, who loved them. So when she again became pregnant, it was with some anxiety that she presented herself at Katie's pre-natal clinic. Was it inevitable that her children would all be in some way deformed?

Katie made her usual examination, asked a few questions about diet, and came to a simple conclusion. There was a vitamin deficiency here. So she produced some vitamin tablets, gave careful instructions as to

when they were to be swallowed, and in due course
Martinho held in his arms a bouncing baby son who was
without a single defect in his sturdy little body. From
that moment on Martinho held Dona Caterina Legg in
the highest esteem, and retained a life-long confidence
in the efficacy of vitamins.

The success of her treatment helped to impress the
Campos family on Katie's mind, too. After years in the
medical work at Rusitu, where she knew scores, if not
hundreds, of patients by name, she had to start to build
up relationships all over again in Mihecani. Her task
was the more difficult because, never having learned
Portuguese, she now had to study it as best she could.
Fortunately, one of the assistant male nurses spoke the
same tribal language she had used at Rusitu, and this
proved sufficient for medical purposes. It was not
without some pride in his wife's achievements that
Gordon, in the annual report for 1956 on the work in
Mihecani, recorded 2,000 treatments per month, and
136 deliveries in the maternity ward during the year.

The hospital, of which she was in charge when the
Staffords left, was a comparatively small affair. It
consisted of a single-storey building, rather like a
bungalow, at one end of which the daily clinic was held,
with a ward for maternity cases at the other. Here Katie,
assisted by the two Africans whom she and Vere Stafford
had trained, and two assistant midwives, dispensed
medicines and good advice, applied poultices, bound up
broken bones and delivered babies who, like babies the
world over, usually arrived at night. The delivery of a
perfectly formed baby to the wife of Martinho Campos
was not the only success that established her reputation,
but being one of the earlier ones it made a special
impression.

But the clinic and the maternity ward was only one
department of busy Mihecani. There was the Church,
with its Sunday services and weekday meetings to be

conducted, and visits to be made to outstations. There was the Bible School, to which some twenty men from the outstations came for six months at a time, leaving their land for others to cultivate while they were away. If the little groups of believers, scattered over hundreds of square miles in the bush, were to be nurtured in the Christian life, there must be men trained in the Word of God, to be their pastors. The great commission of Jesus Christ, prior to His ascension, was not only to preach the Gospel to all, but also to make disciples. One of the most important contributions that John Stafford and Gordon Legg made to the work in Mihecani was the extending and developing of the Bible teaching that had already been started by John Proctor.

And then there was the school. The school, it seemed, was always likely to be the target for official opposition. It provided for the Africans that which they could obtain in no other way for their children – education in the Portuguese language. And without that education, what chance would they have of practical advancement? So the Africans from the outstations flocked to Mihecani with their children, and the school grew and grew. Then, as groups of evangelical believers were established in outlying areas, branch schools were established in four of them. Things were going swimmingly for the evangelical schools. Their reputation was spreading far and wide – so much so that the Roman Catholic authorities began to take notice.

They took prompt action. Quite suddenly the four outstation schools were ordered to be closed, and no amount of protest or persuasion could change the edict. The order was obeyed, and in a short time four Roman Catholic schools were opened instead. Only Mihecani school remained, apparently secure with the authorisation granted years before by the Provincial Governor.

So what was to be done for the children whose educational opportunities had been snatched away?

After various discussions it was decided to open a
boarding school in Mihecani to which they could come.
Courteous approaches were made to the authorities for
permission to take in boarders. But then another snag
appeared. Permission had been granted for the
Evangelical Mission to run a day school for the Africans
in Mihecani, but there had been no mention of a
boarding school, it was pointed out. Permission was
refused. The people in the north who wanted the best for
their children saw no way of obtaining the longed-for
education.

It was at this point that Amisse, who lived in the north
himself, provided the answer.

Amisse was a slightly-built man, with features that
resembled those of the Arab mariners who had sailed
down the east coast of Africa on their trading voyages
centuries before. His cheekbones and nose distinguished
him from his neighbours, with their broader, flatter
features, as did his quiet manner and industry. He had
planted large gardens and tended them carefully, and
although he never became a wealthy man, as Gordon
Legg commented:

'He was dedicated to whatever task he undertook,
and always seemed to add that little extra which made
his house, the roadway to it, his garden, even his chicken
house, more attractive and better finished than others
around him.' He was a spiritual leader to the little group
of believers where he lived, and a man to be relied on. If
only he would be prepared to go down to Mihecani and
run a sort of hostel for the children whose homes were
too far for them to be day scholars! It would mean being
away from his home and family for months on end,
leaving his gardens for others to tend, and seemed
almost too much to ask. But it was not too much for
Amisse. He agreed to the suggestion, made suitable
arrangements for affairs at home, and became the
warden of a newly-built village of thatched huts off the

Mission property in which some sixty boys were housed
for nine months of the year. His example and
industrious spirit gave the boys a good start in life –
better, probably, than they would have had in any other
way. Many of them became steadfast Christians, and a
strength to the Church in the dark days that lay ahead.

One problem having been overcome, another
presented itself. The authorities asserted that the
academic qualifications of some of the teachers in the
school fell below what was required, and they must go.
The missionaries were faced with the difficult task of
replacing them. Two elderly men who had retired were
brought back, and somehow the classes continued. But
there was always the uncertainty of what official
restriction would next be put on the work. The
Portuguese officials, the plantation managers and the
traders were generally very cordial towards the
Evangelical Mission, and Gordon and Katie had some
good friends among them, as they were to find out later,
in the time of their greatest trial. But the Italian fathers
in the Roman Catholic Mission less than a mile away
were in almost open opposition, and they had the upper
hand where the civil authorities were concerned.

There were times, however, when the Italian fathers
went too far, as in the case of the burning of the church,
or 'Prayer House', at Retxua, some sixty miles away.

The first Gordon knew about it was when he and
Katie, sitting at breakfast one morning, looked out of
the window and saw two men cycling towards the house,
whom he recognised as men from the Chapala area.
'What has brought them here so early?' he exclaimed.
'They must have started yesterday and cut across
country, and spent the night in the bush somewhere.'
He got up quickly and went to meet them. 'Good
morning, Fernando,' he said. 'Good morning, Vitorino.'
Then, noting their agitated expressions, he asked, 'Is
anything wrong?' The fact that something was very

wrong soon became evident, for Fernando, by-passing
the usual preliminaries that custom demanded, came
straight to the point.

'The priest has burnt down our church!'

'Burnt down your church? A priest?'

'Yes! He came early yesterday, and went to Chief
Retxua and ordered that our church be burnt down.
But Chief Retxua refused. He said the church was the
house of God, and he couldn't do a thing like that.'

'Chief Retxua said that?' Gordon was rather
surprised. He knew Chief Retxua. He was an old
Mihecani schoolboy, who had done well in his exams,
and whose behaviour had been good, but he had never
given any evidence of personal faith in Christ. It was
heartening to learn that, probably out of respect for his
teachers and the education he had received, he had
taken such a definite stand.

'Yes, he said he wouldn't do it, and the priest was
furious. He called a small boy and ordered him to bring
fire at once. The boy was terrified and ran off to get a
burning stick and gave it to the priest, who pushed it
under the thatched roof, and the church burnt down in
no time. We just stood there, looking at it – our church.'

Gordon could picture the scene. The dark-skinned
Africans standing almost paralysed in the clearing,
silent except for the sharp intake of breath and a
murmured groan as the flames shot upwards, crackling
and carrying bits of burning stick and thatch into the
air. The Italian priest in his long black gown,
contemptuously casting away the stick with which he
had set the blaze going, and stalking away to get into his
car and drive off. Then the dismayed consultations
together, the moans and tears of the women, the sighs
and despairing gestures of the men, the efforts of
Fernando and Vitorino to rally hope and decide what
must next be done.

'So we decided to come straight to you, and tell you

about it', they explained. This was a matter better dealt with by a Westerner, whose word carried more weight with the authorities than that of an African. So here they were, looking at him now to see how he would react.

'All right', said Gordon. 'There are a few things I must see to first, but then Dona Caterina and I will get into the truck with you, and get to Chapala this very day.' A short time later they tied the two bicycles on the back of the truck and climbed up into it themselves. Martinho Campos, now one of the elders of the Mihecani church, accompanied them as an evidence of fellowship with the distressed little congregation. The journey took about two and a half hours, for the gravel road was in better condition than usual after a spell of good weather. On arrival they heard the whole story over again from Chief Retxua himself, embellished by excited comments from the crowd that had gathered. Then followed a viewing of the devastated church, of which little remained but some charred rafters and burnt grass.

Gordon was sobered by what he saw, and by the bewilderment and discouragement of the little group of Christians as they stood looking at the blackened heap of burnt timbers in the heap of ashes. This was all that was left of the church they had built so enthusiastically and sacrificially, and in which they had congregated with such joyous fervour to sing the choruses and recite the verses they had been taught, to listen to the preachers who visited them from time to time – and in which they had prayed to the living God who had sent His Son to be their Saviour.

And now this had happened. It was a shattering blow to their faith, and as he stood there with them, the midday sun beating down upon the clearing, he realised this was a crisis in their spiritual lives. With their limited knowledge of the Bible and its teaching on death as the precursor of resurrection, of the indestructibility of the work of God, they were in danger of losing heart. Now was the time to enlighten them, nerve them for what might yet lie ahead, and assure them of ultimate victory.

'We will stand here and have a little service,' he said. 'Our church building has been destroyed, but it was only a thing of wood and thatch. The real Church of God is in our hearts, and nothing can destroy it there. God's Church has always been persecuted, but has it been wiped out? No! It has grown. History proves again and again that the Church grows in times of persecution. Why, we read in the book of Acts that when the believers in Jerusalem were oppressed and scattered by the Jewish leaders they went everywhere preaching the Word. And so the good news of salvation was spread abroad. The Apostle Paul, writing to the Philippians from prison in Rome reported that his imprisonment had all worked out for good, and that as a result of it many of the brethren had become stronger and bolder in their witness. Throughout Church history the same thing has happened' – and he cited two or three instances that came to mind, all pressing home the point.

'The enemies of Jesus thought they had finished Him when they hung Him on the cross, and saw Him die. But had they? No! He rose again three days later, and they could do nothing to hinder Him then. He was alive, and He is alive for evermore. And what is more, it is in times like these that the Lord is especially close to His own people. "When you pass through the waters, I will be with you, and they shall not overflow you. When you pass through the fires, they shall not hurt you."' Gordon repeated the promises with glowing conviction, and reminded his listeners that our faith has to be tried, that it may shine out like gold. There was so much that could be said on the subject of persecution and its outcome, that he scarcely knew where to stop. But he had said enough to put fresh heart into the discouraged little group. He was very thankful that he had not allowed anything to hinder or delay him from coming. It had not been in his schedule, but it was of primary importance to come at such a time, to let that handful of bewildered believers see that they were not alone in their trouble, and to reassure them with the promises that God has given of His presence and His power to bring good out of the evil.

When eventually he and Katie climbed back into the truck, Martinho with them, he smiled encouragingly at the little group that stood watching as he slipped into gear and moved slowly back onto the road. But then his face became stern, and he held the wheel firmly as he headed, not straight for home, but to Alto Molocue, the nearest Portuguese administrative post, to see the Administrator.

It was not often he called there to lodge a complaint. He usually went to pay a courtesy call, to ask permission for something or other, giving due respect to the government of the country in which he was residing. But this time it was different. He had come to make a full report of what had happened in the village of Chief Retxua, in Chapala. A church connected with his duly authorised mission, built by the law-abiding African people themselves, had been deliberately burnt down, for no reason at all, in broad daylight, by one of the Catholic fathers. Yes, he knew who it was. The people in the village had given his name, which Gordon now passed on to the administration. The Administrator shook his head disapprovingly as he made a note of it, observing that this sort of thing should not be allowed to continue. 'I am very sorry about it, Senhor Legg. It shall be reported to the right authority.'

So the report, passing thorugh various departments, eventually landed up on the desk of the Bishop in Quelimane, with an official remonstrance at the behaviour of one of his priests. The Bishop, annoyed, sent a message to the culprit, demanding his appearance at the Palace to give an account of himself. When he arrived, after a long journey in a crowded truck, he got a thorough dressing-down.

The Bishop, undoubtedly, understood his dislike of the Evangelical heretics, and did not approve of their activities any more than he did. He would be glad to see the back of them. But to set fire to one of their buildings, in the face of the resistance of the head man of the village, was ridiculous. It put the authorities in a difficult position. Senhor Legg was the citizen of a friendly nation, his mission had been granted leave to have its centre at Mihecani, was duly registered, and had done nothing to contravene the laws of the country. In fact, Senhor Legg was very meticulous in observing rules and regulations, and the Africans who unfortunately had accepted his heretical teaching had a right to build what they called 'prayer houses' if they wanted to. It was beneath the dignity of a Catholic father, appointed by His Holiness the Pope, to go around setting them on fire and burning them up. There were better, far more effective ways of getting rid of the heretics than that, and when the right opportunity presented itself, out they should go. Meanwhile, it was senseless to go beyond the law in opposing them.

The priest in question left the Bishop's Palace in a very subdued frame of mind. He made his way to the bus station, got on the transport truck that would take him on the first leg of his journey home, and found there was only one other passenger on it.

It was Senhor Legg himself.

Which of the two men was the more surprised and taken aback at this utterly unexpected encounter it would be difficult to say. Gordon had come to Quelimane on mission business, and to buy some groceries. To find himself on his way home sitting alongside the very man who had so deliberately destroyed the church at Retxua was embarrassing, to say the least. The atmosphere was strained, and the conversation distinctly cool. But as the truck jolted along, the awkward silence was broken by the priest himself, who turned suddenly to Gordon, saying:

'Senhor Legg, please forgive me burning down that Protestant church. I hate you heretics,' he continued frankly, 'but the Bishop called me to his Palace yesterday and told me I should not have taken the matter into my own hands.'

But Gordon was not prepared to accept the apology too easily. There was a deeper truth at stake, and it was with this in mind that he replied:

'Senhor Padre, God is the One to Whom your confession should be made. He is the One whose forgiveness you need, for He is the One to whom we must give account for our actions. And as we read in the First Epistle of St. John: "If we confess our sins, he is faithful and just to forgive us our sins, and to cleanse us from all unrighteousness."' He struck at the heart of the difference between the Gospel that he proclaimed and the penances the priest would have demanded had the position been reversed.

The doctrine of God's free forgiveness to the penitent sinner who acknowledges his guilt was not what the priest wanted to hear. He didn't want God brought into the matter at all. His apology was merely on the human level, and his only response to Gordon's remark was a grunt. He was obviously relieved when the truck reached the place where he was due to alight and his handshake with Gordon was lacking in cordiality. The incident served only to spread a very thin veneer of friendliness over a relationship that remained fundamentally antagonistic. The Roman Catholic hierarchy in Portuguese East Africa was actively opposed to the Evangelicals, and the arrival near Mihecani of a contingent of nuns made this evident. They had been

brought from Portugal to strengthen the Roman
Catholic work in the area, and their black-robed figures
were to be seen from time to time flitting in and out of
homes on the plantations where they were reverently
received by the Portuguese owners and managers.

Although the Evangelical Mission and the Roman
Catholic Mission were less than a mile apart, they had
nothing to do with each other. The Leggs and their
fellow missionaries knew less about what went on within
the walls that housed the nuns than did the Africans who
worked in their grounds. The cars in which the Italian
fathers travelled along the road were a common enough
sight, but rarely was there any salutation from the
occupants. Night travel was unusual, so when, one
evening, the sound of a car speeding along the road was
heard, it caused eyebrows to rise, especially as, about
half an hour later another car, and then another, roared
by. 'Wonder what's happening at the convent,'
observed Katie. But it was not until the following day
that they learned, from an excited African, that one of
the nuns had eloped.

'Sister Clementina has run away! She's gone off with
a man! She escaped by car last night... The Fathers
raced after her, but she got away...!' How she had met
anybody to elope with in the sheltered life of a nun in
such a remote area was a mystery until it emerged that a
young compatriot, a Portuguese architect, had been
commissioned to see about some alterations or additions
in the convent. Somehow he and Sister Clementina had
seen enough of each other to fall in love and plan her
elopement. He had whisked her away to some of his
relatives living in a town fifty or sixty miles away, and
they had been married in a registry office in Gurue. The
whole affair provided material for gossip and speculation
for weeks among the Portuguese traders in the district,
as well as the Africans. Just imagine! A nun! What
about her vows? But eventually interest died down, and

Gordon and Katie thought mistakenly, as it happened, they had heard the last of it.

It was during this period that Martinho Campos began to have pains at the back of his head – then in his chest – then in his back. Then one of his hands became slightly paralysed. He went from hospital to hospital, sometimes travelling long distances and staying for as long as three months, in the hope of obtaining healing, but it was all unavailing. No one seemed able to diagnose his condition. His general health was visibly deteriorating, and one Sunday, feeling strongly that they should go and visit him, Gordon and Katie set off for his village. They found him, very depressed, lying on a mat on the floor of his hut. He made a feeble effort to raise himself, out of respect for his visitors, but soon sank back, listening listlessly as Gordon read a passage from the Bible, then prayed with him. He seemed like one who had given up hope, and Gordon and Katie, after a murmured consultation, turned to his wife and said,

'Lucia Alminda, why not encourage Martinho to come and spend a few days in the Mission clinic? We have no highly qualified doctors there, but we would care for him and pray for him. Bring him to the Mission, and let us see if there is anything we can do for him.'

So Martinho was brought into one of the huts kept for visitors, and it proved to be the turning point for him, not only physically, but spiritually. No special treatment was given him, only Katie's kindly nursing care, but he was prayed for constantly at the church meetings, and one night, lying alone on his bed, he had an experience he could never clearly describe, but which he never forgot.

'The Lord healed me,' was all he could say, but the memory of that night brought tears to his eyes when he referred to it more than thirty years later. The pains that had been dogging him ceased suddenly. There was a resurgence of vitality in his body, clarity in his mind, and a quickening in his spirit. Life flowed in where despondency and deadness had reigned, and the following day, as he was seen standing and smiling outside his hut, the word quickly got around that a miracle had happened, and Martinho was healed. His physical strength increased daily, and within a short time he returned home, walking briskly and eager to take up his family responsibilities again.

A few days later he and Lucia Alminda made a special journey to Mihecani.

'We want to see Dona Caterina,' they announced. 'We want to thank her for all she did for Martinho.' Katie modestly disclaimed any responsibility for what had happened: 'The Lord healed you, not me. It was a miracle', she said; and Martinho agreed.

'But because you are a nurse and have a clinic here, and could look after me, I came. And then all the brothers and sisters prayed for me, and God heard their prayers, and He healed me. But you nursed me, and I've come to thank you, Dona Caterina, for all you have done for me and my family.'

Something else happened that day. Martinho, to quote his own words, gave himself to God. God had healed him in order that he might serve Him. This was the realisation that was impressed on his mind, and he responded without any reservation. He had been healed in order that he should serve God. 'Since then, I have never thought of any other work.'

He set about preparing himself for whatever that work might be by enrolling for the Bible School. This consisted mainly of lectures and Bible studies in the evenings, leaving the days free for the students to earn their own living. For Martinho this meant teaching in the school in the morning, and helping in the church office in the afternoon. It also involved practical experience in evangelism and follow-up work in the remoter regions. One of those journeys was of a rather poignant nature which linked the distant past with the still distant future.

Gordon had received a letter from a Miss Murray in Cape Province, South Africa, containing an unusual request. Years before, during the First World War, she had been engaged to a young missionary from Scotland who was conscripted by the British Forces to serve with African troops in the north of Portuguese East Africa. Territory there had been annexed by invaders from Tanganyika, and it was during the fighting that young padre Napier had been shot at by a sniper, and killed. Now, forty years later, Miss Murray wrote:

'Would it be possible for you to visit the grave of Mr. Napier and scatter some cosmos seeds on it, in remembrance of our courtship?'

Gordon's willing response to her request was prompted not only by human sympathy, but by a deeper conviction that the visit to that lonely grave would lead to the fulfilling of the commission Christ gave His disciples nearly two thousand years before. It was in an area where, so far as he knew, the Gospel had never yet been preached. It would be difficult to find, for it was some hundreds of miles from Mihecani, but it so happened that Martinho's brother was employed as a male nurse in the Government clinic at the end of the road leading to the district. So Martinho, along with three or four other church elders, set off in the Landrover with Gordon, confident that his brother would be able to direct them to the village nearest to the place they were seeking. After driving for some hours they came to the end of the road, literally, and there stood a large hut with the words 'Portuguese Government Clinic' over it. Martinho's brother emerged to greet them as they slid down out of the Landrover.

Yes, he knew someone who could lead them to the grave of the English padre. It was a long way off, and they would have to walk, as there was no road through the forest for the Landrover. They should make for Chief Mahatche's village, and spend the night there.

The walk, lasting several hours, led them between blackened trees laden with ashes which splattered down on them as they walked, single file, behind their leader. There had been a vast bush fire which had burnt up the whole area, leaving it black and dry and devastated. They were glad when their leader turned and told them they were near their destination, and a short time later they met some African women who directed them to a little clearing where was a simple cross and a tablet bearing the name of padre Napier. They stood round it for a few minutes, heads bowed as Gordon scattered the cosmos seeds, and set off for the village of Chief Mahatche.

As they approached the village one of them noticed a hut in which white tablets containing words from the Koran could be seen. 'A Muslim,' he murmured, and stopped to speak to the man inside. 'We're going to Chief Mahatche's house, and we'll be holding a meeting there tonight. Will you come?' But the man refused. He was a follower of the Prophet Mohammed, he said, and it was the Prophet, not Jesus, who had received the final revelation from God. So the messengers of the Crescent had reached this place before the messengers of the Cross! It was a challenging thought and was reinforced by something Chief Mahatche said later. He had received them with customary courtesy, and listened intently as they related the truths of man's sinfulness, and the love of the Creator, the Great One, in sending His Son to be man's Saviour.

'The Son of the Great One, named Jesus, was killed by wicked men, who nailed His hands and His feet to a cross of wood, and left Him there to die. When He died they put his body in a grave. He was dead, and they thought that was the end of Him. But the Great One raised Him from death! He came back to life! And never, never will He die again.

'He is greater than all the spirits you are afraid of, who harm you. He will only do you good. Believe in Jesus! If you believe in Jesus, you can pray to the Great One, and He will hear your prayers and forgive your sins, and the evil spirits cannot control you any more!'

For two or three hours, one and another of the visiting team preached under the starlit tropical sky, surrounded by curious villagers grouped about the great log fire. Gordon was the one to speak last, and when he had finished Chief Mahatche leaned forward and said:

'These words are good to hear. How long have you known all this about the Great One?'

African nights are never really silent. The incessant humming of insects, the croaking of frogs, the distant cry of a hyena, provide a background of sound to which the ear becomes so accustomed it would be almost frightening if it were not there. It was the same that late evening in the village of Chief Mahatche. The background noises continued unabated, but there was a sudden silence as the villagers and the visiting team listened to the conversation between Gordon and the Chief.

'How long have you known about the Great One?' The question hung in the night air, demanding an answer, and Gordon replied:

'Since I was a child. My parents knew it, and their parents before them. We have known it for many, many years in the country I come from.'

The Chief looked him straight in the eyes, a rather strange expression on his face. Then he came out with the second challenge of that memorable day.

'Why is it you have been so long in coming to tell me and my people about Him?' he asked.

7

'We wrestle...'

'"Why have you been so long in coming?" That is the question that has rung in my heart many times since Chief Mahatche put it to me.' Gordon paused, looking out over his audience, then continued, 'And I have thought of those who, over the years, might have gone, but for one reason or another failed to do so. Perhaps there is someone here, even tonight, who is closing the ear to the call of God. Does the challenge of that African chief's question stir you?'

Gordon was speaking at a public meeting, two or three years later, when he and Katie were back in Britain for their furlough. As he went around the country, reporting on the progress of the evangelical faith in Portuguese East Africa, he drew on personal experiences to bring home to his hearers their own responsibility. And he had some challenging stories to tell of Africans living deep in the bush whose hearts opened readily to the message of God's love when they heard it. He told of one of the times when he and Katie were trekking in the north, and came to a village where the Gospel had never before been preached. They decided to stay there for the night, and when he started preaching a crowd soon gathered.

His face glowed as he re-lived the thrill of telling those who had never heard before that God had sent His only

Son to be their Saviour because He loved them. That
Jesus had died to save them from everlasting death, and
that He could save them, here and now, in this life, from
the malignant power of the spirits they feared so much.
But his voice dropped to a lower key as he related what
the headman said wistfully as they were leaving:

'Will these good words that we have just heard for the
first time ever come again and remain in our village?'
Were they to hear only once in a lifetime? But because
there were not enough workers, Gordon could make no
firm promise to that headman. There were too many
other villages to be reached, and the work he was doing
at Mihecani, the Mission's only centre in the whole
country, must remain a priority as far as he was
concerned. It was at Mihecani that evangelists were
trained in the Word of God, and it was from Mihecani
that they went out to proclaim the Gospel, turning off
the main roads to follow the little paths that ran off into
the forests and the bush, where innumerable villages lay
hidden. It was in the African evangelists, trained at
Mihecani, that hope for the evangelisation of the whole
region lay, and it was of them that Gordon spoke again
and again in the meetings he addressed while home on
furlough.

'I suppose it costs the Mission a lot to support them',
people sometimes enquired innocently, and Gordon was
prompt to correct that impression.

'No, the Mission doesn't support a single African
evangelist. Our aim has been the establishment of an
indigenous church in Mozambique, quite independent
of foreign money. We didn't want to encourage "rice
Christians", whose livelihood depended on us. These
evangelists are given a small monthly payment from
church offerings, through the church treasurer, but rely
mainly on the harvesting of the crops in their own
gardens. To a great extent they are honorary workers.

'We *do* subsidise Bible and hymnbooks. They are so

expensive to produce the Africans simply could not afford to buy them, and more than anything else we want them to have the Word of God. But even these we sell, at a price within their means.

'We missionaries are supported by money from our home countries, of course. Christian friends and church groups contribute towards the Mission. And of course we do evangelistic work as well as Bible teaching. But our main work is Bible teaching, for the best means of evangelism is really through the African believers themselves.

'And what joyful reports these evangelists bring back from time to time, telling of ways in which God is working beyond anything we could imagine!'

One of the stories Gordon had to tell was of a gramophone record in a local language which Senhor Cornelio used in a village where he had no other way of making himself understood. Senhor Cornelio was the Portuguese-speaking African employed as teacher at the Mihecani Primary School and his thoughts, from time to time, had been directed to some villages eighty miles north of Mihecani. Eventually, believing God was urging him there, he cycled with another African to the area, armed not only with Scriptures in Portuguese and leaflets in local African languages, but also with a gramophone and some specially produced Gospel records as well. Some Indian storekeepers bought some New Testaments, and the leaflets were eagerly taken by labourers, but it was the gramophone that attracted the greatest attention among the local Africans.

'Here is a machine that speaks our language!' Excitement ran high, and more than excitement. The words that had been recorded were charged with power, and spoken with conviction. Some of the listeners, men who had heard the message before, and responded to it, but then drifted back into their old manner of life were suddenly arrested. Those words in their own tongue, coming so clearly over the night air, spoke to their hearts. They were reminded of the Invisible One who had freed them from the power of evil spirits, of Whom they had heard that He died for them, and as that happened they were ashamed, remembering actions that they knew to have been wrong.

'Like the prodigal son, tired of wandering in the far country, they returned to the Father's house,' said Gordon, using the Biblical illustration familiar to his listeners, and then went on to report that many backsliders came back to the Lord, confessing their sins and praying for forgiveness, as the result of listening to those Gospel records. And that was not the end of the story. One of them had recently been made headman of his village – an added responsibility that carried added influence, too. An opportunity to use that influence occurred almost immediately, for while Senhor Cornelio and his companion were still in the neighbourhood, the headman one night heard the sound of drums which he recognised as being made for a dance to the spirits. He went to investigate, and found about two hundred people gathered, watching while some danced frenziedly around a sick man. This was the time to take advantage of his position, but he needed that gramophone to make the best use of the opportunity. Hurriedly he cycled off to borrow it, and when he returned, set it up with an air of authority, turned the volume up to full, and started the record playing. The crowd, hearing words spoken clearly in their own language, apparently coming from nowhere, suddenly stopped their crooning and listened intently. The dancing ceased, the drums were silent, only the voice was heard proclaiming peace of heart and forgiveness of sins through faith in Jesus. Then an old woman exclaimed loudly:

'That word is just what I have been wanting. From now on, I believe in Jesus!' while an old man said:

'How foolish to try and appease the spirits by

dancing! If the Great One has sent His Own Son, hasn't He done all that we need?'

The outcome of that evening with the gramophone was that many who listened to it set off next morning to find the evangelists and beg to be told more...

Then the evangelists moved on again, and reached a village that had been specially impressed on Senhor Cornelio's mind. Here again, the Chief received them gladly, and called all his people to come and hear what they had to tell. There was a brief interruption while they were speaking, a young man in the crowd suddenly announced that he had heard all this before, but he had not told anyone about it.

'Then you should be ashamed!' said the Chief sternly, turning to him. 'You have heard these wonderful words before, these words that tell us that the Great One loves us, that we can pray to Him, calling on Jesus, and He will hear us and help us! You have heard these words, and you have kept them to yourself? You do not well!'

Gordon paused at that point, and said slowly:

'Perhaps the thought came to you as it comes to me – do we deserve the same rebuke the Chief gave to that young man? Am I, are you, keeping this good news to ourselves? Is the Chief of chiefs saying to us – "You do not well"?' His listeners were not allowed to sit back in complacency, listening to thrilling stories about the conversions of Africans far away in the bush, as though those stories were irrelevant to their own lives. And not all his stories were thrilling ones, either. Some were very moving, like the one about the man who arrived one day at the door of his office, with the request, 'I want to buy a Bible.'

Gordon looked at the man, and knew what he was asking for. There was no complete Bible to be had in the Lomwe language, but the New Testament and Psalms had been translated and produced by the Bible Society, and they were in great demand. All the stocks had been sold out weeks before, and there was not one copy left.

'I'm so sorry to disappoint you,' said Gordon. 'We've had some on order for months, but they haven't arrived, and we're sold right out.'

The expectant expression on the man's smiling face changed slowly to dismay and then dejection as the news sunk in. 'Not one? Can't you find even one for me?'

Gordon shook his head. 'I'm so sorry. Not one left. We haven't had any for weeks.' Then, not recognising the man, he asked:

'Where do you live?'

'I live in Napeiua's village,' was the reply. 'And it took me two days to get here. Oh, I do wish you had a Bible for me . . .'

Two days' journey through the bush – only to be disappointed at the end. It was not that the Bibles had not been ordered, nor was it that they had not been despatched. An order had been lodged for 250 of them, and they had been packed in five packages and duly sent off. But somehow they had gone astray. One consignment landed up in Swaziland, where a friend of Gordon's found it, and re-directed it. Another arrived in Kenya, where someone, recognising what it was, took delivery, re-packed the fifty books into small parcels and sent them all off by registered post to Mihecani. Gordon never found out who that anonymous benefactor was. A third package arrived, but when opened it was found to contain nothing but old newspapers and cardboard. The books had all been taken out. The other two packages disappeared altogether, and no trace was ever found of them. African after African had to be turned away with the disheartening explanation that though the Bibles had been ordered, they had not arrived.

'We are often reminded that we are fighting an unseen enemy who is very powerful', said Gordon rather grimly, when recounting such incidents. 'The prince of darkness has his ways of preventing the Word of God from reaching those who are hungry for it. He is very active. He has reigned for so long in that part of Africa, holding the minds of men in bondage, and he knows that the entrance of God's Word brings light and liberty.

'Oh, he is active! He knows how to stir up trouble for those who want to follow the Lord Jesus, as some of our brethren living in the bush know. My wife and I went on one occasion to a preaching post some one hundred and sixty miles to the south, and while I was talking to Manuel, the leader, Katie was chatting to Alfredo, who had welcomed her very warmly, specially glad to see her because he had benefited through her work in our little hospital.

'"Have you brought any Bibles?" he asked eagerly.

'"Bibles?" she replied sadly. "We haven't had any Bibles for a long, long time."

'"Oh, I hoped you had your Landrover full of them!"

'"Why would you want so many? What would you do with them?" she enquired. She was quite unprepared for the answer.

'"I would bury them. I would bury them where no one knew where to find them. Then, when the priest came to search our house and destroy my Bible, I could go out after dark and dig up another one. In that way we would not die of hunger for the lack of this good food."

It happened some time afterwards that this same priest complained to the Portuguese Administrator, saying that the heretics continued to propagate their religion, and that it must stop. He demanded that Alfredo's church, where Manuel had been the leader for many years, be closed. All the elders and many men, twenty in all, were called to the Government Administrator, and a case was prepared against them. This resulted in their being sent to prison. All their Bibles and hymnbooks were confiscated. The men suffered greatly in captivity, then, after a time, they were sent to work on a scheme to bring a supply of water to the town, under the direction and supervision of a Government engineer.

'Well, I was concerned for them, and asked permission to visit them, and this permission was given', Gordon continued. 'After the usual greetings and general conversation, I asked the engineer if he would permit me to speak to these men, and he readily assented. He said he had never had such a group of prisoners who worked so hard, were so respectful and co-operated so well with him. What a privilege it was to give them a word of encouragement, assure them that God was in control, and would enable them to fulfil their tasks honourably. I also added that the light of the Gospel could not be extinguished by the imprisonment of God's people. The engineer stood by, listening, and although he made no comment, I could see that he was surprised.'

Gordon had further news of those twenty prisoners to give, and very moving it was. They were released eighteen months later and sent back to their villages. They had suffered for their faith, but were all the stronger for it, and when church services were re-commenced people flocked to them. And that was not all. Forty miles away, near the town where the men had been working as prisoners, four more groups of enquirers met weekly to attend meetings that were held for them, to which Gordon himself went to preach from time to time, accompanied by evangelist Manuel.

'Look at that water tower!' said Manuel, pointing to the tower that could be seen in the distance. 'We Christians worked hard to bring water to Mocuba when we were prisoners. Pray that we may work even harder now, to bring the Water of Life to this town, and all around.'

'What a witness to the power of God in the lives of those African brethren!' exclaimed Gordon. 'And that was not the end, either of their spiritual fruitfulness or of their suffering.' And he went on to recount what he had heard and seen on a further visit made to them. Martinho Campos had been with him on that occasion.

'How are things going here?' he had asked. 'What has been happening lately?' He had been given a broad grin by Alfredo, to whom he was speaking, and then had listened to the latest event, and its outcome.

There had been a wedding of two young Christians to which a large number of people had come. After the wedding ceremony, with all its joyful singing, followed the Lord's Supper. 'We remembered the Lord Jesus, and His love for us, and how He had suffered for us so long ago.' But what the elders of the church had not realised was that some spies had been in that gathering, and after the Communion service was held Alfredo and three others had been arrested and taken to the Administrative Post.

'There they gave us sixty stripes, thirty on each hand', went on Alfredo, still smiling. Gordon had looked at his hands then, and seen how swollen they were. He knew what form the beating took. It was inflicted with a *palmatório*, a sort of paddle with holes in it which, when brought down sharply on the hand sucked up the flesh, causing bruising and bleeding. 'After that we were sent to prison, all because we had held that Christian service. But how honoured we were!' Alfredo went on quickly, still with that radiant smile. 'Just think! We were counted worthy to suffer for the Lord Jesus, who suffered so much for us!'

'I had no word to say', said Gordon, moved as always at the memory of those swollen hands and that smiling face. 'I was challenged afresh as to my own commitment. These brethren were willing to pay the price of discipleship, and still follow their Saviour, even after such beatings.' And he could tell of one who had paid the ultimate price.

Txiuabo, an elderly man who lived near Quelimane,

had been forbidden to preach by the local authority, but he could not be silenced. He asserted that he should obey God, rather than men, and continued going round the villages in his area, encouraging the believers and preaching the Gospel to all who would listen. Finally he, too, was arrested, and beaten so badly that he fell down unconscious. Then he was dragged to his cell, and three days later he died.

'No wonder the work of God has grown and the number of believers multiplied in these parts! It still remains true that the blood of the martyrs is the seed of the Church.'

*   *   *

It was an inspiring story that the Leggs had to tell during their furlough of the growth of the Church of which Mihecani was the centre. Stirring news was reaching them too, from the young missionary couple left there, of the activities of some of the African evangelists who were preaching far and wide with zeal and enthusiasm. One in particular, Cornelio, seemed to be endued with power from on high, and there were stories of miraculous healings, in which he figured. Everything appeared to be going according to approved standards, and Gordon and Katie could not account for the heaviness of spirit that began to weigh on them. They felt uneasy. Only later did they learn what was happening in faraway Mihecani.

Here is the gist of it.

Cornelio, who had had a vision in which he had seen the sinfulness of his own heart, had started well. He was already an elder in the church, and after the vision, realising that unconfessed sin was hindering his spiritual life and effectiveness, he had asked forgiveness of those he had wronged or accused unjustly. He also restored some stolen property. Restitution was required, as well as confession. His zeal and determination to put things

right had influenced others, and before long it was
evident that revival blessing had come to the Church.

But then things took a strange turn. Cornelio began to
assert authority over others, claiming special revelations
from God, and to take extreme measures in dealing with
what he believed to be cases of demon possession. He
was reported to have trampled on young children who
were supposed to be demon possessed, and which he
claimed were expelled by this method. At this point the
civil authorities took action, and he was taken to Alto
Molocue for questioning. There he was examined by a
doctor, who declared that he was a schizophrenic. After
a course of injections, lasting three weeks, he was
allowed to return home, and although the Provincial
Governor permitted him to continue preaching, said
that he could not have more than thirty people present
at any one service. Cornelio contravened this order, and
held large gatherings at his home at night. It was
obvious that matters were getting out of hand, and the
young missionary couple wrote to the General Director
of the Mission, asking him to come and deal with the
situation. Cornelio seemed impervious to any advice or
reproof that was given to him. But before the arrival of
the General Director Cornelio had caused the death of a
child for the purpose of proving to the missionary and
others who did not believe him, that he had been given
certain powers, which he would prove by bringing the
child back to life.

It would have been bad enough for the evangelical
cause in the country if it had happened in Cornelio's
own village. As it was, the disaster was crowned by the
fact that the murder took place in the Mission
dispensary. The Leggs were urgently requested to
terminate their furlough and return as quickly as
possible to Mihecani. By that time news of what had
happened had reached the ears of the Provincial
Governor, and through him the Portuguese Government.

8

Close the mission!

Cornelio had been arrested, tried and sentenced to twenty-eight years' imprisonment by the time the Leggs arrived at Mihecani. The shock of what had happened was still reverberating through the district, for the news had spread rapidly to the little groups of believers scattered in the bush and in the plantations, right up to the railroad and beyond.

Cornelio was in prison, charged with murder! Cornelio the great leader, the prophet, the man of the Spirit, the worker of miracles! Cornelio who had called so many to repentance, whose fiery words had inspired so many! Cornelio who, it was reported, could even raise the dead!

But he hadn't raised the dead. The child he had killed was dead and buried, the police had come and arrested Cornelio, and now what would happen? Those who had looked on Cornelio as their leader, almost as an angel of God, were completely bewildered. That his own pride and ambition had opened his mind to Satan's deception and had led to his downfall they could not understand. As the General Director said, when reporting on the tragic case:

'Because of the near background of deep heathenism, to many African Christians the line of demarcation between the old and the new is not as clearly defined and understood as we often suppose, particularly in relation to the spirit world. Though we tell the people that God's book, the Bible, is the standard and guide for all Christians, the average African will far more readily follow a man than a book,' adding reluctantly, 'Even if the man goes wrong.' And since the majority of the African believers north of the Zambeze had only small portions of the Bible, if any, the task of Bible translation and teaching was seen to be even more urgent.

'God has done a great work at Mihecani', he went on firmly. 'And even though the enemies of the Gospel have been given cause to blaspheme, that work is living, and will grow in depth and reality in the hearts of many.'

They were prophetic words which were to be amply fulfilled in the years that lay ahead, but it was not easy for Gordon and Katie to see how it could happen in those dark days after their return to Mihecani. A cloud seemed to have settled over the work, especially in the remoter areas a hundred or two miles away. 'The church was shaken to the core', wrote Gordon of that time. 'Individuals were mystified. Satan, the great deceiver, had been at work, and terrible dishonour came to the name of the Lord Jesus, and the work of God as a whole.' But he had no inkling of what it would lead to, or the extent to which Mihecani was to become nothing more than a name, an empty shell in which only a few crumbling buildings remained. The local Administrator was known to have asserted that he would get the Mission closed down, and thereby gain promotion. Gordon knew that much from some of the Portuguese agriculturalists in the district, from whom he heard it. But when over a year had passed since the tragedy, and things were returning to normal, it seemed that the threat was an empty one.

The first intimation of what was in store came over the radio, as Gordon and Katie were eating their supper one evening. They had tuned in, as usual, to the World

News from South Africa, and were listening quietly as
the announcer said:

> This is the Springbok Radio, South Africa. The
> World at 7 p.m...
>
> In the north of Mozambique the Portuguese
> Government has closed a Protestant mission station.
> The Government says the missionaries there are
> fulfilling no useful purpose, and are not having a
> civilising influence.

Then the Springbok radio announcer passed on to
report other items of news, leaving Gordon and Katie at
the supper table looking at each other in a stunned
silence, until one of them ejaculated:

'Mozambique – but that's the name they give this
country!'

'A Protestant mission station in the north of
Mozambique – but that's us!' There was no other.
Hundreds of miles south of the Zambeze several
Protestant denominations* had their centres, but in the
vast northern territory there was only one – the
S.A.G.M. centre at Mihecani.

'Closed! By the Portuguese government!' They could
not believe that they had heard aright. How could the
Springbok Radio in South Africa have information
concerning them of which they themselves knew
nothing? Early the next morning Gordon went to see the
local Administrator, and the response he got to his
enquiry was not reassuring. The Administrator pre-
varicated, saying he had heard nothing, but that if it
were announced on the radio there must be some truth
in it. Four days later Gordon received the copy of a
statement in the Government Gazette which read:

---

*These included Anglican, Free Methodists, Swiss Presbyterian, Church of
the Nazarenes, and the Scandinavian Independent Baptist Union.

'Resulting from an administrative enquiry, it has been verified that the presence and operation in the Province of the *Missão Evangélica de Nauela* are destitute of civilising action. The Governor-General commands – the Mission is extinct.'

Events moved quickly after that. Portuguese and other European neighbours had already rallied round after hearing the news, to see what they could do to help and twelve of them wrote letters testifying to the value of the work. Gordon was advised to go to the capital and with the help of a qualified advocate prepare an 'exposition' to be presented, along with the letters, to the Governor-General.

Excerpts from this document provided convincing evidence of the civilising influence of the Missão Evangélica de Nauela, which had been in existence for 46 years, and included such facts as:

1959   400 children in the kindergarten
            240 children in the upper school
            44 students out of 47 had passed their
            final examination.

In recent years 560 students had passed their final examinations, having been prepared by qualified teachers registered by the Inspectorate of the Education Department. Some of these were to be found in the service of the State, others in private employment, working as interpreters, nurses, foremen, rudimentary school teachers, mechanics, agriculturalists, drivers and soldiers.

In the realm of medicine during 1959 the number of patients helped in the clinic had been 6,377, while 203 babies had been delivered without the loss of a mother. In the same period 1,150 women had attended the pre-natal clinic including the wives of Portuguese and Indian neighbours and public functionaries. In addition, there had been 408 dental extractions.

But before this 'exposition' could be even presented to the Governor-General, things had come to a head. On the Sunday after the news had got around of the statement in the Gazette, Africans began coming early in the morning from all quarters to attend the service. The long low building with its impressive facade of twin towers was soon filled, men standing in the aisles and at the back, overflowing into the porches around. When Gordon arrived to conduct what proved to be the last Sunday service in the church at Mihecani, he saw men from the outstations, parents of school-children, people who had been patients in the clinic, local sympathisers, all gathered in bewilderment and questioning to swell the usual congregation of some three hundred to about two thousand. Gordon was not a man who readily displayed his emotions, but as he stood to deliver his sermon his chest was constricted and a lump rose in his throat. He announced his texts, from Peter's First Epistle, and read:

> Dear friends, do not be surprised at the painful trial you are suffering, as though some strange thing were happening to you. But rejoice that you participate in the suffering of Christ...
>
> And to the elders among you... Be shepherds of God's flock that is under your care... 1 Peter 4: 12, 13a, 5: 1a, 2.

He was in the middle of the sermon he had prepared when suddenly he was interrupted. A man rose to his feet and called out:

'Senhor Legg!' It was Jacinto Vieira, the headmaster of the school. Gordon paused, looking at him questioningly, and the man continued, 'Senhor Legg! Should you not ask all the elders to stand, and commend them to God at this time?'

It was a moment charged with emotion, and as the elders rose to their feet a deep hush fell. There were fourteen of them, all men Gordon knew and trusted, men who had stood firm through the storm that had raged after the Cornelio affair. He glanced quickly from one to another as they stood, dotted among the congregation, their faces turned solemnly towards him. The elders from the districts around – Manuel, Luiz, Dunquene, Amone, Simiao, Davide, Moises. Those from the central church – Abilio, Bernardo Braga, Rodrigo, Leonardo, Mendonça, Eduardo – and Martinho Campos.

The stage was set, not by man's arranging. There could scarcely have been a more dramatic or impressive manner of handing on the torch, of passing over the responsibility for the evangelical church to African leadership, than when Gordon stood, that Sunday morning, and committed the elders to God, and they solemnly accepted their charge. If the official handing over did not take place until years later, the Divine commission was surely received then. For him the experience was almost overwhelming. This was the end to which not only he, but every other member of the Mission who had worked in Portuguese East Africa had been looking. Their aim had been the establishment of an evangelical church in the country that was self-supporting, self-governing, self-propagating. On this Sunday morning in September, 1959, he was seeing with his own eyes its accomplishment.

But how different it all was to anything he might have envisaged! This was no pre-arranged ceremony, carefully planned with Mission leaders and African pastors to mark the joyful beginning of a new era. This unrehearsed event was being forced on him by circumstances beyond his control. On the face of it, hostile powers were arrayed against him, and were prevailing, and he would have been more (or less) than

human had he been unmoved by the realisation that this
would probably be the last time he would stand there
preaching to the congregation in Mihecani. Among the
vast concourse of Africans gathered, the prevailing
mood was of anxiety and gloomy apprehension. The
Mission had been a centre of healing and education, as
well as of Christian faith, for as long as many of them
could remember. It was part of the background of their
lives, and they could not conceive what it would be like
to be without it. For Gordon the emotions of exultation
and worship were mixed with those of human grief and
dismay, as the ominous clouds of uncertainty hung
threateningly over the future.

Three days later they broke irrevocably. The local
Administrator arrived with his assistant and said:

'Senhor Legg, I give you twenty-four hours to close
down your Mission. Please empty all the premises, lock
the doors and hand over the keys. My workmen will seal
all the entrances.'

*   *   *

Twenty-four hours! Twenty-four hours in which to
disband a school of seven hundred pupils and a staff of
over thirty. Twenty-four hours in which to close a busy
dispensary, to send home half a dozen pregnant women
in the maternity ward. Twenty-four hours in which to
pack the medicines, the books, the office files, clear the
workshops and the garage, to say nothing of their own
home and personal belongings.

And what about the staff?

Gordon and Katie felt stunned. It had not occurred to
them that the edict would be carried out so suddenly
and drastically, but it was evident from the implacable
expression on the Administrator's face that he would be
quite unwilling to modify his order. Katie's thoughts
flew to the two huts in which five orphans were being

housed and cared for. 'But what about the children – they are orphans, they've got no parents. We look after them here . . .' she said, and her eyes filled with tears as he replied:

'You'll have to send them away and find another place for them to live.' He went on eating, for having delivered his ultimatum he had announced that he and his assistant would stay for lunch. But he had the grace to observe, as she surreptitiously dabbed her eyes with her handkerchief.

'At least I can see how much your wife cares for the people . . .'

The Leggs were noted for their hospitality, but never was it extended under such strained circumstances as at that luncheon table, and Gordon could not refrain from saying sternly and clearly:

'Sir, you can close down this Mission station, but you can't close down the work of God in the hearts of the Christians here.' The Administrator looked rather surprised at that, and had nothing to say in reply. When he had finished his meal he got up and went to instruct his workmen to seal up the doors when they were locked, and took himself off.

How they got through the next two or three days, Gordon and Katie never knew. The time limit of twenty-four hours had to be extended, not because the Administrator relented, but because the wind time and time again blew out the flames of the little lamps with which the workmen were melting the wax to seal the doors and windows. It was obvious that they would not be able to finish the job by sunset so the dead-line was extended to forty-eight hours. During that time Gordon and Katie worked almost ceaselessly, day and night, sorting papers, burning some and packing others, distributing school desks and benches to those who could use them, disposing of furniture, sorting medicine and equipment, making arrangements for paying off the staff, talking to the many callers, especially the elders of the church who wanted to know what could be done to maintain the meetings and services, now they were suddenly without a church.

'Crowds came to share their grief with us,' wrote Gordon later. 'But one thing struck us forcibly. Instead of the people asking for clothing, furniture, medicines or other things, the only thing they asked for was copies of the Lomwe New Testament and Psalms. "You cannot go and leave us without Bibles" said one, voicing the thoughts of many. The few that were kept in the wards for the use of patients were handed out and as Katie and I each had one we decided that we could manage with one between us, and give the other away.'

What they themselves were to do, where they were to go, they did not know. 'We've got the Landrover', they said to each other. 'We can sleep in that, if necessary.'

But that was not immediately necessary, though it was later on. A friendly Portuguese trader not only agreed to store all the bales and packages that were piling up outside the locked premises, but he cleared a room at the back of his shop, and put it at their disposal. 'You can stay here as long as you like', he told them. So when the church and the school-rooms, the dispensary and the maternity wards, the kitchens and the living quarters of the Mission station at Mihecani were all locked and sealed, they looked round he deserted clearing which only two days before had been thronging with life, climbed into the Landrover with all their baggage, and drove away.

For six weeks the room at the back of the Portuguese shop was their home. They went off in the Landrover day after day, visiting remote villages where they knew church members lived, holding impromptu Bible studies, encouraging parents distressed that their children's school had suddenly been closed, praying with the elders who came anxiously to see them to discuss what could be done now.

One of those visits stood out in Gordon's memory years after all the others had dissolved into the mists of the past. Martinho Campos had come, along with three of the other elders, and they were huddled together in the back room behind the trader's shop, talking about the situation.

Things were looking grim, and the consultation, like most of their consultations in those days, was a solemn one. The evangelical church had received a crippling blow with the closing of the Mission at Mihecani. What was in the future for it, thinly spread as it was over hundreds of square miles? They could only surmise, and questioning arose as to what were the spiritual lessons to be learned from the apparent disaster. Martinho was not one to take the lead, for he was by nature a rather retiring man, and conscious of his educational limitations. But on this occasion he spoke with conviction, though his contribution to the discussion was based, not on his own ideas, but on something he had heard in one of Gordon's sermons.

'Senhor Legg', he said. 'You were telling us some time ago that the church needed cleansing. You were saying "Judgment must begin at the house of God."'

'1 Peter, Chapter 4, verse 17,' murmured Gordon and waited for Martinho to continue.

'And you explained it by a bicycle tyre that had been punctured, you remember.'

Gordon shook his head. He did not remember, but it was the type of simple illustration he would have used. The Africans with bicycles knew all about punctured tyres.

'Go on,' he said, and Martinho continued,

'You showed us an inner tube with several punctures, and you told us that it would be no use patching the hole until we'd cleaned the tube. You reminded us that we had had to rub hard sometimes, even using emery paper to get the dirt off, and that if we didn't it would be a waste of time to stick on new patches. The glue wouldn't hold. We knew that, of course, but then you said it was all like a parable. There are times when the church is like a bicycle with a punctured tyre. The air has escaped because something has pierced it. One of Satan's darts has injured it . . .' It was not difficult for the listeners to identify such a circumstance with the Cornelio affair, though Martinho did not mention it. 'And you said that it must be cleansed before it can be mended and made fit for use again, and that it may be a painful process. Like emery paper grating on the inner tube . . . But it's sometimes the only way.'

Then Martinho fell quiet again, and left without any further remarks when he departed with the others. No one knew at the time what was going on in his mind. It was not until years later that he divulged what he believed was God's call to him to take the lead in church affairs.

'I knew that God had chosen me to do this, and I could not understand why. I could not understand why He had chosen me . . .' It is doubtful whether anyone else would have understood, either, at the time. Martinho was just one of the steady, reliable elders of the church, with nothing outstanding about him. Like most of the other elders, he had started holding quiet Sunday services in his own village for the few believers there, but they were very small. None of them dared to hold big meetings. The Portuguese authorities had forbidden it.

Meanwhile, Gordon and Katie were preparing to move. The Administrator was making things difficult for the friendly trader, and for his sake they knew they must find accommodation elsewhere. Again a Portuguese acquaintance, this time an engineer on one of the tea plantations, came to their rescue.

For six months after the closure of the mission station at Mihecani they lived in this way. They moved sixteen times during that period, travelling from place to place in the Landrover, heartened by the hospitality of Portuguese settlers and the generosity of African believers, who came again and again with their gifts of food – eggs, a chicken, potatoes, vegetables. Day after day they set off to visit quietly in the villages or on the plantations, responding to requests for help.

'Dona Caterina, please will you look at my little boy. He's getting so thin, and won't eat. Can you give him some medicine?'

'Senhor Legg, this tooth is hurting me so much. Can you pull it out for me?'

'Senhor Legg, what was that story you told us about the son who went away from home and wasted all his money?'

'Senhor Legg, teach us that chorus again – the one about Jesus dying for us...'

Everywhere they went, it seemed, there were those who wanted to listen to more of what was in the Bible, to learn hymns and choruses, to pray. The church elders managed to keep in touch with them throughout the whole period, especially Martinho Campos and Braga, who arrived sometimes after dark to report what was happening. The Roman Catholic fathers were rounding up the children and insisting on them enrolling in their schools. Some parents had refused to let them go, and had been imprisoned. This little church and that little church had been burnt down. In very few places now were the believers holding their Sunday services openly.

The evangelical church was going underground. But it was not dead. The words of John Donne, written in different circumstances and in a different country and in a different age were as applicable to the church in Mozambique in the latter part of the twentieth century as they were to him in the early seventeenth century:

> As the tree's sap doth seeke the root below
>   In winter, in my winter now I goe
> Where none but Thee, the Eternal root
>   Of true love I may know...

When Gordon and Katie, in response to a Mission directive, eventually crossed the border into South Africa, in the winter of the church they were leaving they knew that sap remained in the tree.

9

Martinho to the Fore

Colonialism in Africa was coming to an end. Smouldering fires of resentment at the white man's domination were bursting into flame with country after country claiming independence, and names being changed. Nyasaland became Malawi, Northern Rhodesia became Zambia, Belgian Congo became Zaire. Kenya retained its name but discarded its colonial status, and even in Rhodesia white rule had to yield in the end and lower its flag to see Zimbabwe's emblem hoisted instead.

The Portuguese territories could not escape. Angola, on the west coast, started its war of liberation in 1961, and a year later Portuguese East Africa was slipping into world news as Mozambique. Mozambique had been classed as a province of Portugal since 1951, and an infinitesimal percentage of Africans accorded civil (though not political) rights as 'black Portuguese'. It was these 'assimilated persons' who began to form nationalist groups in 1960, hopeful of a more or less peaceful transfer from Portuguese to African authority. They soon discovered that such hopes were without foundation. The result was the creation of Frelimo (*Frente de Libertação de Moçambique*) and the start of a guerilla type warfare which was to bring a reign of terror, particularly in the remoter areas of the country, which lasted for years.

The Leggs left for furlough in 1960, and were refused
permission to live in Mozambique when they re-entered
in 1961. They were told their reason for dwelling there
no longer existed. The Mission had been closed. They
were instructed to leave the country immediately, and
the permanent residence papers Gordon had held for 22
years were taken from him. They must apply for a
consular visa if they wished to re-enter the country. In
consequence no evangelical missionary society remained north of the Zambeze. The Scandinavian
Independent Baptist Union, operating in the far south,
was invited to supervise the work, and this arrangement
eventually resulted in the formation of the Igreja Uniao
Baptista de Moçambique. These official moves proved
of great value later on, but at the time did little to help
communication between the churches in the south and
what had been the widespread, flourishing church
centred in Mihecani, hundreds of miles away in the
north. As far as Gordon Legg was concerned, the
curtain had gone down on the scenes and the people on
whom his whole missionary career had been centred. He
and Katie had to adjust themselves to an entirely
different style of life, in the thickly populated, bustling
city of Johannesburg instead of in the African bush, and
to a different type of service, too, for he had been
appointed to work at the headquarters of what was now
the Africa Evangelical Fellowship [A.E.F.]. The
changing of names, a feature of the second half of the
twentieth century, was taking place in societies as well as
in countries, and the South Africa General Mission was
one of those that realised the old appellation no longer
described it acceptably. For one thing, white rule in the
Republic of South Africa made it an unpopular title in
other African countries, and in any case the society now
had workers in Zambia, Malawi, Zimbabwe, Botswana,
Swaziland, Namibia and Angola as well. It had
outgrown its old title, and the new one fitted it better.

The Africa Evangelical Fellowship it had become.

An evangelical fellowship could grasp opportunities in a rapidly changing world more effectively by not being tied down to a full programme in the old-time style of mission station. And where African leadership was emerging, it was no longer appropriate. With literacy increasing, Bible correspondence courses provided a simplified theological education to men and women who could never obtain it in any other way. Radio broadcasts, unknown to a former generation, required scriptwriters, translators, linguists, if the Christian message was to be disseminated adequately. In comparatively backward countries like Zambia and Angola missionary doctors and nurses were in demand, and everywhere Bible teachers and translators were required. This was perhaps seen as the most urgent and widespread need in all the areas where A.E.F. had its workers. The response of Africans in the rural areas to the Gospel of Jesus Christ was difficult to follow up among people who had very little Christian literature in their own languages, and who, in many cases, could not read it even if they had it.

Gordon, with his long and intimate experience of life in the African bush, knew the situation, and in his new position as assistant Director had plenty of opportunities to promote Bible teaching among the members of the Fellowship scattered in various places throughout the southern half of the great African continent. He travelled to visit them frequently, and seemed immersed in the work of his new role which took him everywhere – except to Mozambique.

He adapted to his administrative role as best he could, but what appealed to him in it perhaps more than anything was the opportunity it afforded to do something for the Africans working in the gold mines. This came about in the first place through Ray Oosthuis, A.E.F. missionary in Soweto township. For

some years he had been concerned about those men in
the mines. The gold mines themselves were prospering,
strung in a crescent for over a hundred miles, from
beyond Johannesburg round to Klerksdorp. Eight to
ten major gold mining companies were operating there,
employing tens of thousands of men who came from half
a dozen Southern African countries on contracts
ranging from six months to two years. Some of the men
stayed on for a lifetime. They were herded together in
row after row of rooms housing twenty to thirty men,
with bunk beds, open coal fires, and very little
ventilation. The food provided was adequate, dished
out to them as they queued up at meal times in the
kitchen, plate in hand, and medically they were well
looked after, for the hospitalisation was excellent when
they were ill.

But what of the spiritual, emotional, mental needs of
these men? Ray Oosthuis rarely saw them, being
unconnected with the mining industry, but he knew
enough about their conditions and activities to be
challenged by what he heard. Drunkenness and
prostitution thrived in their vicinity. The lack of normal
family life, and the change from the living conditions in
the bush to which they were accustomed, exacerbated
the evils. In addition, inter-tribal animosities flared up
among them, invariably ending in fights, sometimes in
murders.

'Human beings for whom Christ died, right on our
doorstep, and we are doing nothing to bring the Gospel
to them.' Ray Oosthuis could not ignore their need, and
wondered what could be done. Then he thought of
Sundays, when they were free. That would be the time
to reach them, visiting them in their dormitories.
distributing tracts and booklets among them, preaching, singing, holding informal meetings. He talked
about it to the General Director, and when Gordon
joined the staff it was decided that the time had come to

set things in motion. Ray Oosthuis and Gordon Legg
were deputed to make a survey of the whole situation,
and having done that to approach the authorities for
permission to start Christian work among the miners. It
would involve a lot of preliminary paper work, followed
by visits to the European managers to obtain their
approval, then approaching the African foremen to
obtain their co-operation.

The whole exercise had an added incentive as far as
Gordon was concerned, for some of those miners would
have come from Mozambique. They were arriving at
the rate of 1,000 a week.

And Mozambique was where his heart was.

He kept in touch as closely as he could by
correspondence with the elders of the scattered church
at Mihecani, and as time passed it became evident that
the quiet, steady, unexceptional school teacher and
evangelist, Martinho Campos, was emerging as its
leader. It was to him that Gordon wrote in connection
with the production of a booklet of Scriptural extracts
on the subject of everyday living. He had been in touch
with Scripture Gift Mission about this, and had received
an assurance that a good supply of these booklets would
be provided without charge when a duly corrected
translation into the Lomwe language had been
procured. This had involved Gordon in weeks of work,
first obtaining the translations, then poring over them to
ensure the correct meaning had been given, and finally
sending the whole carefully prepared manuscript back
into Mozambique, addressed to Senhor Martinho
Campos, for him to check and return. Gordon had taken
special pains to ensure its safe delivery in Mozambique,
taking it personally to the Post Office in Johannesburg
and sending it by registered post. It was a matter of high
priority to him, this production of Bible verses relevant
to practical issues of life anywhere, and he waited
eagerly for information concerning its progress. He was

surprised when he did not hear that the manuscript had arrived, and eventually wrote to Martinho asking:

'Have you received the corrected manuscripts which I returned to you four months ago? Have you sent off the final copy of S.G.M. booklet *Everyday Life*, because it has not yet come to hand?'

A few weeks later he had a reply from Martinho. He had never received the packet, he wrote, but had been making careful enquiries at the post office in Nauela about it. Eventually he had learned that a local post office worker had seen the large registered envelope, concluded that it contained money, and had opened it. Finding that it contained no money, and not knowing what to do with the tell-tale envelope and manuscripts, he had burned the lot.

So that meant doing it all over again. 'It would appear that our great enemy does not want the Holy Scriptures to be distributed in Mozambique,' wrote Gordon feelingly. His early experiences in Chiuangumabvu had left him in no doubt as to the reality of Satanic powers, and he had had no reason to modify his views. They were not manifested so openly in the more civilised regions – that was the only difference.

It was to Martinho that Gordon wrote about the possibility of obtaining copies of the New Testament and Psalms in the Lomwe language, too. It would involve a journey of several hundred miles, down to the capital, where the Bible Society had a depot. It was doubtful whether Martinho had ever travelled so far from his home before but the need for those books was becoming urgent, Gordon was no longer in a position to get them himself, so if someone else did not do it the Scriptures would be denied to hundreds of Africans who were pleading for them. Would Martinho go?

Martinho went. It was a big undertaking for him, especially as he was to make the return journey by air, to which he was quite unaccustomed. But he did it, finding his way through the city with its ornamental, colourful architecture and overhanging balconies, its bicycles and crowded streets, its penetrating smells of garlic and dried fish, to the Bible House, and returning with 250 copies of the New Testament and Psalms, all he was allowed to carry on the plane. It was the first time he had gone to the south as the representative of the church in the north, and provided the opportunity to meet two or three of the African pastors with whom he was to be associated in years to come. Not that he had any intimation then of the role he was to fill in the church nationwide in the future. His one aim at that time was to obtain as many copies of the Scriptures for his own people as possible. He was spending more and more of his time among them, visiting as many as forty homes in a day sometimes, cycling or walking through the bush or on the plantations, to pray, read, preach, not only to believers but to any who would listen. He and the other elders had agreed that they must carry on the work at least by having Sunday Schools for the children and classes for adults, even though they were forbidden to hold Sunday services and similar meetings.

'We must pray', Martinho said. 'We must pray for boldness.' And he suggested that they should get together, for that very purpose. Their guide and pattern was the experiences of the early church as recorded in the New Testament. They had read many times of the imprisonment of Peter and John after the healing, in the Name of Jesus, of the lame man, and how, when they were released, they had gathered together with the other believers, to pray. And what they had prayed for had not been that the authorities would be overruled, or that opposition to their message might cease, or that things would get easier. They had prayed for themselves, and their prayer had been that they might have courage to proclaim God's word, come what may.

'Now, Lord, consider their threats and enable your

servants to speak your word with boldness.' To proclaim
His word with boldness was the task committed to them,
but beyond that they had no power. So they went on to
pray for what was beyond their power to do. 'Stretch out
your hand to heal and perform miraculous signs and
wonders through the name of your holy servant, Jesus.'
They asked God to confirm their words by performing
miracles when the Name of Jesus was involved.

The Biblical record of that event told of the shaking of
the building after they had prayed, and that they were
all filled with the Holy Spirit.

No record remains of the gathering of the elders from
the church at Mihecani, except what Martinho told
Gordon years later. Five of them had come together,
praying earnestly, in the same way as those early
disciples, for two or three days. Whether or not there
were any outward manifestations at the time, indicating
the response of God, Martinho did not say. The
evidence of God's response came afterwards.

*   *   *

One day towards the end of June 1963, Gordon received
a long letter from Martinho. It had taken over two
months to reach him, and he read it eagerly.

It started off with warm thanks for the books, Bibles,
hymnbooks and catechisms that he had sent to them.
'For all we praise God, and pray that He will bless you in
the service of the Lord. We, all the Christians of the
districts of Zambezia and Niassa send many greetings
and Christian salutations.' Then followed detailed
accounts of the progress or otherwise of the work in
various areas, and a list of places where meetings were
being held on Sunday – eleven in the Province of
Zambezia, nine in the far north-western Province of
Niassa. Martinho had visited them all, he informed
Gordon, and added:

'One lack is that of books in every place, because now there are many believers and the Word of God has reached as far as Lugela and Namaroi. I have a desire to reach those parts too, if God will.'

But the main purpose in Martinho's writing was to ask if Gordon could meet him and two or three of the elders, in Malawi. A matter had arisen, very favourable to the Christians, in a place called Ile. It all started with one of the local chiefs arriving, dead drunk, at a meeting the Christians were holding, and beating up the women. The men got hold of him and took him off to the local Administrator to get the matter settled, taking along the pots of beer the chief and his people had been using, as evidence.

'When he saw them the Administrator was furious, and very angry with the chief, snatched off his hat (demoted him) and sent him away. The following day the Administrator called a meeting of all the chiefs and said:

'"I am very pleased with the way in which the Protestant Christians behave, neither drinking nor dancing. In your areas you should accept the message of God and believe the Word of God!" then he said to all the Christians, "I want you to have a meeting and write a letter to the Governor of Quelimane and ask him for permission to have regular meetings in a certain place. And choose a good, moral, honest man to be your representative. Go home and think about it, and then let me know whom you have chosen."'

And now the Administrator was waiting for a reply, and the elders, after consultation, decided they needed some advice. They must ask Senhor Legg.

'For this reason we are writing to you to ask counsel from the missionaries. Matters of this kind which we have to decide between us, elders of the Church, we find very difficult and we do not wish to reply to such a thing without asking counsel of our superiors at Mission

Headquarters.'

The long letter ended on a very personal note.

'I have a great desire to meet you, Senhor Superior . . .
a great desire to go to Blantyre to speak with you face to
face about all that we can do.' And he signed himself,
            'Your humble servant and great friend,
            MARTINHO CAMPOS UAPALA.'

Gordon lost no time in replying, but before any plans
could be finalised Martinho had taken matters into his
own hands. He and two of the elders simply strapped a
few belongings on their backs, set off the couple of
hundred miles to the frontier, walked calmly across the
political boundary which after all, was merely a line
marked on a map, and sent off a telegram from Blantyre
informing Gordon where they were, and asking him to
join them immediately.

The telegram was delivered to the P.O. Box number
of the A.E.F., and arrived at the office along with the
morning mail. Gordon had opened half a dozen letters
before he came on it, and it took him a minute or two to
digest its contents. Go to Blantyre immediately? For him
it was not so simple. There were matters for which he
was responsible right where he was, engagements to
keep, letters to write, meetings to attend. The torturous
journey to Blantyre from Johannesburg would take
three days by train and bus, and there were timetables
to be scanned, forms to be filled in, tickets to be bought.
He had not bargained on moving so quickly when he
agreed to meet them in Malawi.

But they were there already, confident that Senhor
Legg would respond, as always, when there were urgent
matters to be attended to in connection with the
Church in Mozambique. Martinho, Elder Harela and
Teacher Ramos Domingos, waiting for him . . .

'By all means, go!' said the General Director. 'This is
important. We'll double for you here somehow.'

Twenty-four hours later he and Katie were on their way to Blantyre.

*　　*　　*

'Elder Leonardo Coelho of Nauela has gone the wrong way because of putting his sons before God,' said Martinho. The excited greetings between the Leggs and the three men from Mozambique were over. Questions about this one and that one had been asked and answered, messages passed on, and at last Martinho was getting down to giving a report of the work in general. Not everything was going well, and the case of the elder in Nauela was evidence of that. 'It is very sad. His sons all walk in the way of sin, and elder Leonardo doesn't try to stop them. His oldest son was married to a Christian girl, Violetta, with the approval of her parents, in 1960, and the marriage was registered at the *Posto*. Then this son went to Beira and took another woman – a 'coloured' woman, partly European, and elder Leonardo agreed to it. And he did a very bad thing. He took Violetta all alone to the *Chefe de Posto* to try and arrange a divorce. She didn't know what was happening until she got there and he offered to pay her off with a sum of money. But when she understood what it meant she refused the money, and right there before the *Chefe de Posto* said she didn't want it, she wanted the husband she was married to.

'The *Chefe de Posto* was very annoyed with Leonardo.

'Brother Bernardo Braga and I,' continued Martinho, 'we went three times to elder Leonardo to tell him a brother ought not to do such a thing, but he refused to listen to us. The fact is, he wants to keep in line with his son, who is now an "assimilated person", a black Portuguese, and others like him. He wants that honour, and doesn't want to be despised because of the Name of the Lord Jesus Christ. So now he has resigned from being an elder in the church, and has separated from us. We keep on praying for him.'

'What about Violetta?' asked Katie anxiously. She knew the girl, who at one time had been employed in the home of fellow-missionaries at Mihecani. 'Where is she – and how is she?'

'She's back home, living with her parents, she and the child. She's still a good Christian, attending all the meetings, and still waiting for her husband to return to her.'

There was another case of a defecting elder, this time in the Niassa Province in the north, to be reported. This one had been secretly living with a woman whose husband had gone to work in Blantyre. The local chief heard about it, and remonstrated with him, but he refused to give her up, and when her husband returned went along to see him privately and offered him money to buy him off. However, the husband took the money to the local chiefs and indignantly told them the whole story, which soon got around, to the dismay of the Church elders. 'What shame on the Name of the Lord Jesus!' The outcome was that the other elders decided he must be disciplined, no longer allowed to take any active part in the work of the church.

'But the remainder of the elders continue in the way of the Lord, and believers in Nampula are asking for baptism.' All told, the good reports far outweighed the bad ones, and it was evident that in spite of the shortage of Bibles and New Testaments, in spite of the limited experience of preachers and teachers, in spite of the continued opposition of most of the Roman Catholic priests, the number of evangelical Christians was increasing. And the very defections that Martinho reported in detail were evidence of their general good behaviour, and that drunkenness and immorality were not tolerated among them. This was especially notice-able in the Ile district, where the Portuguese Administrator had expressed his approval.

'You chiefs must respect the Protestant church,' he had said firmly when he called them together after the incident of the drunken attack on Sunday morning. He was prepared to encourage the Protestant church to be officially recognised in his district, once their representative had been chosen.

As Gordon talked and prayed with Martinho and his companions, and gave them his advice, his mind went back to Mr. Claridge's lonely grave so short a distance away. '"Except an ear of wheat fall into the ground and die, it abideth alone. But if it die, it bringeth forth much fruit." What's happening in Ile now is evidence of that,' he said. That life laid down, the human sorrow of the courageous young widow, had not been in vain. And as he listened to all that the three men had to tell him, acceded to the request they had to make, he marvelled at the quality of their Christian discipleship.

'Senhor Legg, we've got some money we want you to keep for us,' they said, producing several little bundles of grimy, tattered bank notes. 'This is from all the church collections. It's to be used to support the evangelists when they take time off from their own work to go out preaching. We're afraid it may be confiscated if we try to put it in a bank in Mozambique. Can the missionaries in Blantyre keep it for us? Then we can draw it from them when we need it.'

So that was arranged, but there was yet another financial matter they wanted to discuss. It had to do with the Christmas offerings. It had been their habit to give the whole of this to Christian work in another country. One year they had sent a donation to help work among the blind in Malawi, another year for leprosy work in Zambia, another year for a Worldwide Evangelization Crusade launch for river evangelism in Guinea Bissau. Now that Senhor Legg was not there to tell them about God's work in other countries, they did not know what to do about the Christmas offerings.

He pointed out that the Bible Society had work in many countries, including Mozambique. It would be quite a simple matter to give a donation to the Bible Society next time Martinho went to buy more New Testaments for the Christians in Mozambique.

What he did not suggest, and what took him by surprise, was their insistence on paying his return fare. He remonstrated, but they would take no refusal. After all, he had travelled to Malawi at their invitation, they said. Besides, he had often told them it is more blessed to give than to receive. They wanted that blessing! He must take the money.

There was no answering such an argument. Deeply touched, Gordon agreed to accept it. So, that matter satisfactorily settled, the three men, with broad smiles, said goodbye, and turned back to trudge over the border into their own country.

10

Martinho Reports

Martinho was leading a series of meetings in the administrative area of Gurue, some sixty miles west of his own
area of Nauela, when he was arrested. It was
humiliating, to say the least, to be bundled along with
the other two preachers into a police van and driven off
like any common criminal to be clamped in jail without
a trial. Martinho had all his life been one to keep within
the law, and this was not a pleasant experience. He was
treated differently from the others who were arrested
with him, too. They were placed in a common cell, but
he was put into solitary confinement, where he had to
remain in ignorance of what was going on outside,
where he was very inadequately fed, and what made
things even worse, was given no washing water.

It was not that no one was concerned for him. The
Christians who had been attending the meetings,
knowing the prisoners would be dependent for food on
what was sent in for them, came along with sacks of
flour, far more than was needed. The supply was so
great that the Chief of Police, a European, noticed it and
made enquiries. These must be unusually important
Africans, he thought, and it was not without reason that
he was suspicious. The rebellion against the Portuguese
domination had started with the formation of Frelimo,
and recruits for guerilla warfare were being secretly

mobilised. For all he knew, those meetings the three
men had been leading might have fallen into that
category. However, even when he learned that they
were merely what the Roman Catholic priest called
gatherings of heretics, he made no move to release them,
or even bring them to trial. He had other matters on his
mind, and there was no knowing how long Martinho
and his companions would have had to remain in jail
had it not been for the vision he saw as he was driving
along the road one night. He was in a truck with a
warder and half a dozen prisoners whom he was taking
to another area, when suddenly he saw what appeared
to be a man in gleaming white, standing in the road,
facing him. Swerving and braking violently to avoid the
vision, he turned the truck over, and was trapped
underneath it. The prisoners themselves heaved it off
and released him, and a motorist in a passing car took
him home. From there he had to go to hospital in
Quelimane for treatment for his injuries. What was in
his mind all this time was the vision he had seen, and the
realisation that it was linked with his treatment of
Martinho. On his return to Gurue the first thing he did
was to go to see Martinho in his cell, and ask his
forgiveness. And when Martinho spoke to him about his
need for the forgiveness of God, he said humbly:

'Please pray for me.' So there in the dingy, filthy cell,
heads bowed, the unshaven, unwashed African prisoner
prayed earnestly for God's forgiveness and blessing on
the European standing so meekly before him.

When Martinho told Gordon about the experience,
some time later, he spoke little of his sufferings in that
lonely cell, but one of the things that stood out in his
memory was the action of the Chief of Police
immediately he had prayed for him. It was almost
exactly what the jailer did for Paul and Silas after the
earthquake in the Philippian prison. He called for hot
water, that the prisoner might wash. Martinho never

forgot that humane little episode, and the relief that it brought. His suffering was over now, for the Chief of Police took him out of solitary confinement, ensured that good meals were provided, and went off to arrange for a proper trial. He called all the local village chiefs together to see if they had anything against Martinho Campos and the two who were arrested with him. Only one of the chiefs was against them, and he was a notorious drunkard. His opposition spoke more forcibly in their favour than would have his approval, had he given it.

The three men were released immediately, and the outcome of the whole affair was beyond anything Martinho would have hoped for. Not only did the Chief of Police make plain his respect for what he stood for, but granted him official permission to travel throughout the whole area under his jurisdiction, in order to preach and hold evangelical services. Martinho had already applied for, and obtained this permission in his own area of Alto Molocue – now it was extended farther afield.

God was evidently leading him into wider spheres of service, and from time to time the means he used were clearly miraculous. The deliverance of the demon-possessed girl was a case in point. This took place in Niassa Province, at Nante, where paganism and Islam were both well rooted, and where there was only one small group of people who asserted they believed in Jesus. Martinho had gone to visit them and to hold meetings, teaching them hymns, preaching and praying. They had gathered in the little church they had erected and Martinho was already preaching, when in came a young woman of about twenty, wild-eyed and unkempt, whose appearance immediately distracted the others.

'It's Maria, daughter of Cabai!' they whispered to Martinho. 'The spirit within her drives her. She goes around crying, running around. Her father can't control her, doesn't know what to do with her. It's the demon inside her...'

Martinho went on preaching and the girl squatted down with the others, listening. After he had preached he prayed, and at the end of the prayer she suddenly called out:

'Oh, Jesus, save my life! Oh, Jesus, save my life! Oh, Jesus, save my life!' Then she fell over on the floor and lay there silent. But after Martinho had prayed for her she stood up, looked round quite normally, and spoke rationally. The change was dramatic in its suddenness – too dramatically sudden for her mother to believe it was for the good. When she went home and quietly offered to do some cooking, her mother looked at her and gasped in a frightened voice,

'Oh! She's got another demon!' There seemed no other explanation for the altered manner and appearance. Maria herself had the explanation, which at first mystified them. 'Jesus has saved me', she asserted. 'I'm a Christian now.' Her parents did not know who Jesus was, and Christian, to them, was just the name of a foreign religion. But there was no denying that whoever or whatever Jesus was, He had freed their daughter from the power within that was making life for her and for them, a miserable and agitated existence. The preacher, Martinho Campos, was evidently the one who was in touch with this Jesus, just as the witch-doctors were in touch with the spirits whom they could call on, and the thing to do now was to go and see him, and take a suitable gift to ensure his good services in the future. They decided on offering him money, and went along with 3,000 M.T. (about £75) to give to him.

To their surprise, Martinho refused to accept it. He explained to them that the evil spirit that had been tormenting their daughter was not cast out through any power of his. It was Jesus, the Son of God, who had driven the spirit out. Then he went on to explain that

Jesus heard the prayers of all who believed in Him – it was to Him their daughter had prayed when she called out 'Jesus, save my life!' and He had heard her. His power was far greater than any of the spirits who haunted and horrified men, driving them, as poor Maria had been driven. Maria had called on Him to save her, and everyone could see the result. Martinho did not fail to tell them how Jesus, God's Son, had been nailed to a cross of wood, and had died on it, been buried – but three days later had come to life again, never to die any more. He had died for the sins of mankind, taking the punishment due for their wrong doings on Himself, and God had raised Him from the dead, for He Himself had done no wrong. Now He was in the place of power, at the right hand of the Most High God, and there was nothing He could not do.

Maria's parents had never heard all this before. There were a few people in the neighbourhood who said they were Catholics, but they did not talk like this. It sounded good but was it true? But as the days passed, and Maria remained as rational and cheerful as the first day when she had astonished them by offering to do some cooking, they agreed that they wanted to believe in this Jesus, too. Before long a little church had been erected where they lived, and more names were added to the growing list of adherents to the evangelical faith.

Then there was the breaking of the drought in the district of Pebane, in Zambezia Province. The people there, pagans and Muslims alike, had been doing everything they could think of to induce the spirits to send rain. Animals had been sacrificed, money, food, garden produce had been ceremoniously cast into the lake time and time again, and still the heavens were brassy, the earth dry and cracked.

Eventually the chief called on everyone in his district to come together to worship the spirits and offer more sacrifices. It was to be a united gathering, from which no one was exempt.

But the Christians, few as they were in number, steadfastly refused to attend. They could not join in, they said, because they worshipped the One True God, Jesus Christ. He had the power to send rain. They would pray to Him, but they would not sacrifice to the spirits, or cry to them.

The chief was very angry. There had been murmurings already about these people who were not adding their quota to the sacrifices thrown into the lake, and suggestions that this was why rain was withheld. So indignant was the chief at the Christian's outright refusal to obey him that he took a few of them and would not let them return home, virtually keeping them prisoners. When the local Administrator, evidently a fair-minded man, heard about it, he called the chief to come and see him, and said:

'Why not let these Christians get together and pray for rain, and see if there is anything in what they say about their God?' As the Administrator had the greater authority, the chief had to act on his suggestion. The Christians he was keeping prisoner were released, the remainder joined them, and they met together with as much solemnity as the pagans and Muslims who had gathered by the lake – but not to offer sacrifices to the spirits. They prayed very earnestly, loudly sometimes and with tears, for the matter was urgent. Not only had the need for rain become desperate, but their faith was being put to the test, their God, so to speak, was on trial.

They had never had anything like this happen before, but Jesus, their God, had all power and authority, and He *must* hear their prayer. So to Jesus they prayed. 'Lord Jesus, send us rain!'

And the wind began to blow.

Then little clouds were seen scudding across the erstwhile clear blue sky. The clouds thickened and became darker, and people stood outside their huts, looking up and murmuring with awe that the Christians were praying to their God.

And the rain came pouring down.

It came down in sheets, bouncing off the dry ground, forming pools and rivulets that ran into every slight depression, whipping down branches from the trees and thatch from the roofs while the people, regardless of the damage done to their huts and their fences let the welcome rain beat on their bodies and shouted that it had come at last.

The God of the Christians had heard His people's prayer.

After that the Administrator gave permission for the Christians to hold services anywhere in the district of Pebane.

And it was not the only place in which the European Administrator demonstrated a sense of justice which turned the tide in favour of the Christians. At Alto Ligonha, in Zambezia Province, the chief had treated twelve of the Christians very badly, beating them up and forcing them to drink a highly potent local concoction. When the Administrator heard about it he was extremely annoyed, and calling the chief to appear before him said:

'God is a God of justice, and you will punished.' Then he had a mug of the mixture handed to him and said, 'Now *you* take this and drink it, and see how you like it!' So the chief had a taste of his own medicine, and the result was alarming. He came out with an itch all over his skin, especially on his legs, which became very inflamed and painful. They irritated him so much he had a boy with him to administer a primitive form of first aid – the boy had to scratch where the chief indicated he itched. It was about three years before he was clear of the condition, and during that time the witness of Christians in the area was having its effect. Many people were attending the meetings, and

eventually Martinho was urged to come and interview
those who were ready to be baptised and take their stand
as Christians. So he went, and when he had examined
all the candidates he announced that twenty-six of them
could be baptised, and that the ceremony would take
place next day in the river.

Now there were known to be many crocodiles in that
particular river. There had been a succession of
casualties as women went down to the river to draw
water and when they saw the sudden swirling of the
water were not quick enough to run up the bank. The
news got around that the preacher, Martinho Campos,
would stand in the water and baptise twenty-six people,
so crowds gathered on the banks to see what would
happen. The Christians knew the danger, and prayed
earnestly for God's protection, standing as near the
water themselves as they dared, singing lustily the
hymns that had been chosen as one after another went
down into the river to be baptised by Martinho in the
Name of the Father, and of the Son, and of the Holy
Spirit. He stood there calmly in the softly flowing waters
until the last candidate had been plunged down and
come up again dripping and brushing the water from his
face as he waded back to the bank. Then Martinho
himself waded back – and the waters started swirling.
The crocodiles were coming back.

'Many were praying for me', he told Gordon and
Katie, as he related the incident, and all that had
happened during the years since they had left. 'God is
good, and He hears our prayers', and he continued
telling of the various ways in which openings had been
given to preach in many new places. As they listened
they marvelled, and the next letter they wrote home to
their supporters started with the words:

   ... we were like them that dream.
Then was our mouth filled with laughter, and our

tongue with singing: . . . The Lord hath done great
things for them.
The Lord hath done great things for us; whereof we
are glad.   [Psalm 126:1–3]

The letter was dated Aug/Sept 1968, and it was written
shortly after they had completed their first official
return visit to Mozambique.

There was a two-fold purpose in this visit. One was to
introduce a Swedish missionary, Mr. Pollack, and
Pastor Jose da Conceiçao, of the Union Baptist Church
in the south of the country. They were to shoulder the
responsibilities Gordon had held in Mozambique,
including the spiritual care of the congregations in the
north, and representing them before the Government
when necessary. This was according to the decision
taken by the International Conference of the A.E.F., the
outcome of many discussions and of many prayers, too.
It marked the official merging of A.E.F. churches in the
north and those founded by the Scandinavian
Independent Baptist Union in the south. It was a union
that was to prove of great mutual benefit in the years
that lay ahead.

The second reason, and from the point of view of the
Leggs the far more attractive one, was to meet again the
people they loved in the country itself, the believers
connected with the happy days and years at Mihecani.
Unceasingly over the years they had prayed they might
go back once more to their old field of service before they
died. Now it had happened. Mihecani mission station
itself, they admitted, was like a cemetery, deserted and
still. White ants had done their destructive work on two
of the buildings, leaving them in ruins, while those that
had walls that were still standing were surrounded by
tall grass.

'Gone was its tidiness and well-swept paths, with
many folk going to and fro between the hospital and the

school.' But what did that matter when the lasting quality of the work done in human lives in those days was there for all to see? As they travelled from place to place and were met by smiling, hand-clapping groups of people exclaiming, 'You've come back! God is great! We thought it could never happen!' they alternated between laughing and weeping for joy.

Meetings had been arranged in various places, and they could only spend a day or two in each, but the crowds that gathered were beyond their most optimistic expectations. Boys who had received their education in the Mission schools, mothers with children who had been born in the hospital, men who had attended the Bible training courses, all came swarming round.

'Do you remember me? I graduated in 1957 from school – I'm working as a clerk in a Government office now.'

'This is the baby you brought into the world, Dona Caterina! See how big she has grown!'

'Senhor Legg, my son wants to meet you. He wasn't a believer until two years ago, but now he is so keen, and goes out preaching...'

The greetings and exclamations were accompanied by many and varied gifts. They received in all about seventy chickens, over four hundred eggs, innumerable potatoes and bunches of bananas, and £40 to help cover the cost of petrol, while the women came along with about half that amount as a special gift for Katie.

'The Lomwe people are not very demonstrative or emotional, but at least on the occasion of our visit they were deeply moved, and demonstrated their love for us,' they wrote, and continued:

'Spiritually, there was evidence of much life and growth, not only at the places we used to visit in years past, but in new areas which have opened up to the Gospel during the eight years of our absence, praise God!'

One place they visited came in for special mention. Gordon had often referred to Ile when speaking at meetings home in Great Britain. He had taken a snapshot of the first celebration of the Lord's Supper with the three local baptised believers in that place which was always associated with Mr. Claridge, the missionary pioneer who had died there. 'First fruits of the Gospel', Gordon called that picture when he showed it on a screen. He can have had no inkling of how great the harvest would be within the space of ten years.

'Now there are thirty-six groups of believers in this one administrative area, and about 600 greeted us with much clapping and singing. How deeply our hearts were touched at such a sight, and our lips filled with praise to God ... Our eyes were not dry, as with a lump in our throat we greeted them in the Name of the Lord, and shared the ministry with Brother Conceiçao, who married eight Christian couples during the visit. All too quickly the forty-eight hours passed. We met about 200 at the Lord's table, when one and another were commended to Him ...

'Other groups were waiting for us, and we moved on.'

There were now over two hundred congregations and more than ten thousand baptised believers in Zambezia, and the same number of enquirers. Elders and leaders had been duly appointed to lead meetings, teach Sunday Schools, and generally act as local pastors.

'And the seven school teachers who were taken on at the Roman Catholic Mission along with the pupils after our school was closed by order of the Government, have all refused to attend Mass,' Martinho told Gordon. 'In spite of the priests trying hard to win them over, they have stood firm. And so have the elders in charge of the prayer houses. The priests wanted to establish their own schools at every prayer house, but the elders wouldn't let them!'

The Leggs were only away from Johannesburg for

three and a half weeks, but in that time they had travelled thousands of miles by train and Landrover, and it seemed that all their questions had been answered, and desires fulfilled, with what they had seen in Mozambique. They had even seen the orphans about whom Katie had been so distressed. They had been received into Christian families and were evidently well looked after, including Daniel, so called because, as an infant, he fell from his mother's back and escaped unharmed when she was attacked and killed by a lion.

It has to be admitted that Gordon and Katie retraced their steps to Johannesburg very reluctantly. Their visit to northern Mozambique had far exceeded their most optimistic expectations, with its evidence of a Church that was truly indigenous, healthy and flourishing. It had even been heartening to hear why the Christians were not always popular among their fellow Africans – not among the men, anyway. The complaint was that they only had one wife apiece, and there were times when they actually went to help their womenfolk working in the fields.

For Gordon it had been especially exhilarating to be preaching in Portuguese again, with Martinho interpreting into the Lomwe dialect, and to see the response of so many to the message of the salvation of the soul, free and eternal, through faith in Christ Jesus. It was tough going, of course, what with sleeping on floors or in the front seat of the Landrover at times, much hard travelling over bumpy roads to remote areas, shaking hundreds of hands on arrival and preaching several times a day.

'But it was wonderful!' And on that note the letter was brought to an end.

11

News from Nauela

'And remember, Gordon, you are General Director of the Africa Evangelical Fellowship now,' said the Chairman of the International Council clearly, adding with a little smile and a twinkle in his eye, 'Not only Mozambique'.

The remark brought an understanding chuckle from the other members of the Council, and a murmured reiteration of the words, 'Not only Mozambique'. After several years at the Fellowship's headquarters in Johannesburg everyone knew to which country of southern Africa Gordon's thoughts and affections most readily gravitated. His name was always associated with Mozambique, and even a term of office as General Director of the whole Fellowship was unlikely to alter that. However, his sense of responsibility ensured that all the other duties accruing to his new position were heartily attended to, and Mihecani was far from his mind when the telephone rang one day in his office, and a woman speaking in Portuguese asked for Senhor Gordon Legg.

'Yes – Gordon Legg speaking...' he replied in the same language, and then with amazement heard the voice at the other end of the line announce:

'I am Clementina, the nun who ran away from the convent in Nauela in Mozambique. Do you remember?'

His mind went back to the night when he and Katie had heard the cars racing along the road from the Roman Catholic Mission, and had been told next day that one of the nuns, Sister Clementina, had eloped with a man. It had been the main topic of gossip in the European community for days. Certainly he remembered!

'I was a Catholic then, but I'm one of you now. I'm converted! Let me explain,' and briefly she told her story. She had eloped, hoping she would find in marriage the peace and contentment she had been seeking for years in the Benedictine Order to which she belonged, but although she was happy enough with her husband, inner conflicts had increased. 'I could not sleep. Constantly I was in fear. Everything perturbed me. All things were sin. In the end I became ill and had to receive medical help. I turned back to the "saints" and religious devotions, but they did me no good. Then I tried to become an atheist but in my heart I knew there was a God!'

Gordon listened with a sense of rising exhilaration as she told of someone she met in Maputo who had once been a nominal Catholic but now had a living faith in Jesus, and was radiantly happy, and then of a Protestant couple in Johannesburg whose lives had impressed her. 'There was something different about these people.' They invited her and her husband to their church, and after a time first he, and then she, put their trust in Jesus Christ.

'I knew that what I was hearing was the same as what you had been preaching in Mihecani,' she told Gordon, 'When I heard that you had come to Johannesburg I tried to find you – I've been trying for two years. Then, quite unexpectedly, a printer who had published my story told me he had done work for you, and gave me your telephone number. I was delighted! So I am ringing you. My husband and I would like to meet you.

Could you and your wife come to our home?' So it was
arranged that he and Katie should go and visit them one
evening, and when the time came they set out expecting
to spend a quiet few hours alone with these new
acquaintances. But when they arrived, to their surprise,
and initial disappointment, they were ushered into a
room with about twenty-five people in it – all
Portuguese. They had not expected to be absorbed into
a social gathering among complete strangers. However,
it soon became evident that the ex-nun had planned no
ordinary evening party and that the pleasant exchange
of personal reminiscences could wait until later. She
introduced Gordon briefly as the Protestant missionary
who had lived in Mozambique, near where she was then
in a convent, and that he would be able to tell them all
much more about Jesus than she could, since he knew
Him better. She had invited as many of her Portuguese
friends and neighbours as possible in order to hear him.
What was of primary importance to her was to bring the
reality of Jesus Christ in her life to others, and she felt
that this man who had preached with such effect to so
many Africans in Mozambique must surely be one who
could influence her friends, too.

As things turned out, it was probably she as much as
Gordon who influenced the men and women gathered
there that evening, for Gordon, responding readily
enough to the opportunity provided, asked her first to
tell them how she herself had found peace and joy
through faith in the Lord Jesus.

So it all came out – the early impressions made on her
as a child by her very religious Catholic mother; the
school run by nuns, leading to her own decision to
prepare for a monastic life, and her entry into a convent.

'I tried to practice rigorously all that the Holy Mother
Church imposed, like fasting, making sacrifices, praying, . . . but I never found perfect peace in my heart. In
my anxiety to find the truth I read many books on piety,

and almost all the works of the Fathers, but the Bible
was a totally unknown book to me. From time to time I
had doubts about my choice to be a nun, and spoke to
my superiors about it. I wasn't sure if it was God's will
for me to remain in the convent, I said, but was told that
if I did the will of my superiors I was doing the will of
God.'

Then there came the plunge from convent life in her
own city of Lisbon to convent life in a remote part of
Africa, in faraway Mozambique. She went with three
other nuns to assist in nursing in the Roman Catholic
Mission in Nauela, and was told that the purpose for
which they were sent was to combat the Protestant
Mission in the area.

'To combat the Protestants! In no circumstances
could I ever have supposed then that the day would
come when I would belong to the very people I was
combating!' she exclaimed, then continued her story.
After her elopement she and her husband had lived for
three years in Quelimane, then decided to move to
South Africa. It was while they were staying in a
boarding house in Maputo, en route for that country,
that she was given a booklet by the lady who had once
been a Catholic.

'I was too tired and disappointed with a religion that
gave me nothing but fear and uncertainty to read it at
the time, but when I did I saw that it said the same
things Senhor Legg had been teaching in Nauela.'

But it was through the couple in Johannesburg who
were teaching her and her husband English that her
attention was really gripped. There was something
different about their faith. They really believed God
heard and answered their prayers.

'Strange as it may seem, after this, when problems or
difficulties arose in my life I would stand in my home
and turn towards the church of the Portuguese
Protestants in La Rochelle, and I would ask the God of

the Protestants to help me. And to my amazement and my relief, my prayers were answered. But even after my husband decided for the Lord Jesus, I continued with a very hard heart, very unhappy and with no peace. Then one day, I put God to the test. For the first time I asked God that if He, the God of the Protestants, was real, that He would reveal Himself to my soul.

'And the miracle happened! My life was transformed! From that day, when I truly decided to follow my Saviour, Jesus, my physical and spiritual ailments disappeared. Glory to God! There was just one pain which troubled me and tired me, but on the day that I fulfilled the Lord's commandment and was baptised, this disappeared too, and has never returned. How grateful I am to God for all that He has done for me!'

After that Gordon had no difficulty in proclaiming the message of free salvation, and all that it involved, in this world and the world that is to come. The fact that he had to speak in Portuguese instead of English presented no problem, and it was hours before the guests reluctantly took their departure, leaving the Leggs and the Lourinhos to become personally acquainted. It was the beginning of an enduring friendship between the two couples.

Meanwhile, exciting news was reaching them from Mozambique. Martinho and the other elders had agreed that there must be somewhere for conferences and special meetings, a focal point for all the little congregations spread over the three northern provinces of Zambezia, Niassa and Nampula. And what was even more important, there must be somewhere and someone to whom the Christians in the outlying areas could go with their problems, for encouragement, and to get more Bible teaching. In fact, what was needed was a place like the Mission at Mihecani. So it was decided to build another church in the same style as that at Mihecani. That should be the pattern. They knew what they wanted to do, and were setting about making plans for its erection.

They had no money apart from what came in from their own church collections, but tithing had become habitual and had continued, even after the Mission was closed down. They had no architect or draughtsman, no surveyor or master builder, 'But Paulo Vitxo has had experience in building with bricks, and he will be in charge.' They had no materials but 'we'll make the bricks ourselves, for there are many volunteers'. As for the location, it should be at Eleve, five miles from Mihecani, where Martinho himself lived, with two or three of the other elders not far away.

So in October, 1969, they started building. Teams of volunteer workers from the fourteen congregations in the Nauela area made the bricks, with 300 women and 100 men each working two days a month. Twenty-five men burnt the bricks, and forty more did the brick laying, half of them working two days a week without any pay. Forty-nine carpenters were employed from time to time, as well as men to deal with the 700 packets of cement that were used. And there were roof timbers to be conveyed from the old church building in Mihecani. For all this they had no mechanised transport, except for a truck loaned to them by a friendly European when they had to shift large quantities of bricks.

The whole exercise was reminiscent of the re-building of the walls of Jerusalem in the days of Nehemiah, with everyone who was fit to do so lending a hand. As in the days of Nehemiah there were those who jeered at them, too, wondering at the effrontery of these Africans setting out to erect in the bush a Portuguese-type edifice with impressive-looking twin towers fronting a long low building with colonnades and twelve arches on either side. Added to that there were grim reports of Frelimo activities in the remoter areas, with armed guerrillas descending on villages and terrorising the defenceless inhabitants. Battalions of Portuguese troops were being drafted into the bigger towns and administrative posts, adding to the general sense of tension and uncertainty.

However, nothing daunted the church builders in Nauela. They just went on building. In seven months the church was completed, and they could apply their minds to other matters. A clinic was needed, and church offices, and a school building. There must be accommodation for Senhor Legg and Dona Caterina, and any other missionaries who might come. Furthermore, there must be running water in the house built for them. A tank and some pipes and a tap were obtained, and fitted up so that when the tap was turned water came out – provided, of course, there was water in the tank. But that presented no problem. Some of the men undertook to carry buckets of water and keep the tank filled. And so on. So by the time everything was completed and all arrangements made, the date fixed for the official opening was the first Sunday in November, 1970.

There was more to the occasion than the opening of the church, however. It had been proposed that the Baptist Union in the south of the country should assume responsibility for the churches in the north, representing them before the Government and making annual visits to ensure that evangelical doctrines and practices were maintained. The visit of the Swedish missionary Mr. Pollack, and the Portuguese pastor from Maputo, along with Gordon and Katie Legg, for the church opening, provided the opportunity for the leaders in the northern churches to meet those who would be caring for them in the future.

But before that happened there was a preliminary meeting of the four of them with Martinho Campos in Quelimane. They were to travel northwards together, in Mr. Pollack's Landrover, and there was something symbolic about that journey, for by mutual consent it was Martinho the Mozambican pastor who took the lead. Writing of it later, Gordon reported:

'Martinho Campos had made every arrangement for our visit. We covered thousands of miles, visiting the many major centres.' Martinho had done his organising well. The leaders of each place had been informed what day the visitors would arrive, and how long they could stay, so that all could be ready at the appointed time. The result was, as Gordon went on to record:

'Excited crowds at every place. A hymn of joy to welcome us. Handshakes and greetings from morning till night, as we met three or four groups daily. Many were recent converts... Usually there was rapt attention given when the Word of God was preached. The meetings were always long, for they could never have too much. Often there were 300 to 400 people present, and at one early morning prayer meeting 500 turned up. Several came to the Lord, many were counselled. In spite of much poverty and lack of educational facilities, yet most of them were clean and neatly dressed, bright-eyed and responsive.'

People arrived in various ways – on foot and by bicycle. Here is Alina who looked after the orphans at Mihecani. Here are two of the orphans themselves, tall, rather shy teenagers. Here is one of the male nurses, now a church elder in one of the big sugar estates near the mouth of the Zambeze. Felizardo the driver is another. Maria Rita, leader of the women's work in Nauela. And so on and on and on, old friends to greet in every place and new ones to be introduced, like Augusto, in whose village there are now eighty believers, when four years ago he was the only one.

'Many new preaching centres had been opened, and we were given the explanation for this multiplication. Each believer was encouraged to speak about his faith to others, and wherever one had to walk more than six miles to attend a meeting, it was time to open a regular preaching place in that one's village!' It was all so much

more than he could have envisaged during his years in
Mihecani. There was something miraculous about it.
'The small seed of the Gospel sown in weakness over
many years in Mihecani has not only borne fruit, but its
seed has been wafted by the power of the Spirit into
distant parts.'

Although the visits to the congregations over the
widest possible area, culminating in the dedication of
the newly-built church in Eleve were the primary
reasons for the month-long tour, other calls were made
en route of a very different nature. There were courtesy
visits to be made to the Portuguese administration in the
regions where meetings were held. These spacious,
ornate buildings in the important towns were well
staffed with African police in uniform, while Europeans,
mainly Portuguese, occupied the highest administrative
positions behind big desks in private offices. There was
usually a crowd of Africans waiting to be interviewed, or
to make a petition, and sometimes the little group of
Westerners with Martinho accompanying them had to
wait, too. It was those waiting periods that Katie, in
particular, dreaded so much that she elected to sit
outside in the heat in the Landrover, rather than in the
comparative coolness of the ante-chambers. What she
was likely to see and hear inside the building was too
harrowing, for punishments to offenders were often
enough meted out there in public. So many strokes of
the bastinado on the soles of the feet, so many strokes of
the palmatório on the palms of the hands, with Africans
administering the blows on Africans. The swish-swish of
the paddle through the air, the sharp smack on the flesh,
then the sucking sound as it was drawn off and up, to
descend again and again accompanied by the gasps or
cries of the victim. Or perhaps the culprit was
condemned to inflict his punishment on himself, by
jumping up and down and clapping his hands over his
head for a specified period of time. If he stopped,

exhausted, a policeman was there with a stick to beat
him into action again. It was more than Katie could
endure without showing her horrified sympathy for the
sufferers, whatever their crimes might have been, so the
men went in without her to wait, rather grim-faced, to
be invited in to see the Administrator.

Not that they had to wait long. As Westerners they
got preferential treatment, and having Pastor José de
Conceição himself a Portuguese, with them, expedited
matters even further. Their purpose in going was to be
introduced by Pastor Martinho Campos as pastors of
the duly registered Baptist Union Church. Martinho
himself needed no introduction. The Administrators
already knew him, and acknowledged his presence
courteously. He was evidently in good standing with
them.

And so on to their destination. To gaze in amazement
at the twin-towered church building, a replica of the old
one at Mihecani – to enter the three-bedroomed
'missionary bungalow' and look with tear-dimmed eyes
as the running water system installed for their benefit
was proudly shown them – to protest between laughter
and tears at the gifts brought to them, the chickens and
eggs and goats and a duck, and limitless supplies of
vegetables – to argue in vain about the large sum of
money for diesel fuel for the Landrover, which the
church elders insisted they must accept because: 'We
asked you to come, and it is right we should contribute
to your travelling expenses.'

It was almost a relief to realise that they were not the
only ones for whom generous preparations had been
made. Everything must be ready for the people who
would be coming on the great day. They must have
something to eat! So the Christian women had
undertaken to pound the grain that arrived, sack after
sack of it, till they had some four and a half thousand
pounds of flour stored ready to be used at the right time.

Three thousand Africans attended the dedication

ceremony on that first Sunday in November, 1970, and nearly thirty Europeans as well, local friends who had come to show their interest, and to see the Leggs.

'Will you be coming back to live now?' they asked, but Gordon shook his head. The answer was No, and he knew it was better that way. The decision to leave had not been his, and at the time the closure of the Mission had seemed like a victory for the Satanic foe. Now, eleven years later, it was evident that God had wrought good out of it. 'Life out of death' as Katie exclaimed over and over again, and probably the new life could have come no other way. The Church had always been independent of foreign financial support, but independence of thought and purpose was not so easily achieved. It was natural that its local leaders should lean on the judgment of the foreign missionaries through whom the Gospel of Christ and the Word of God had been brought to them. Furthermore, the immediate presence of a European whose political status put him in a category different from their own with government officials had seemed to be an advantage, however slight and uncertain it proved to be at times. During these past years they had learned deep lessons of direct dependence on God Himself, and the result had been a maturing of faith and a quickening of spiritual initiative.

And God had been with them. There could be no other explanation for the multiplication of believers.

'Never, in the difficult days of long ago, could we have imagined such an increase, but God has done it', wrote Gordon. 'The geographical outreach has been amazing. In the district of Zambezia, about three and a half times the size of Wales, we were told that about 25,000 attend services, of whom 14,000 are baptised, and there are about 300 congregations.'

The greatest need, as always, seemed to be for Bibles. The New Testament and Psalms were the only Scriptures available in the Lomwe language, and the demand for them always exceeded the supply. The leader in one village came to Mr. Pollack with a sum of money equal to that given for the party's travelling expenses, with the urgent request that he provide them with Bibles as soon as they became available.

Hymn books were eagerly bought, too, although at fifty pence a copy for some of the Africans it was the equivalent of a week's wages. But they evidently thought it was worth it, for to stand with those who were singing, faces aglow, and be unable to join in except for tra-la-la-ing the tune was to feel too deprived. Furthermore, hymn books provided additional reading matter, with a rhythm and a rhyming that was very pleasing – very pleasing indeed. So the Africans who had the necessary cash in hand instinctively obeyed the Scriptural injunction to take no thought for the morrow, and bought their hymnbooks then and there.

'There is need for more and more literature, and Saide Braz Chimenha and others are dedicated to the task of translation, which includes another Scripture Gift Mission booklet.' In one way and another men with the necessary abilities, allied to a sense of vocation were emerging. The assertion of the Lord Jesus that He would build His church was seen to be justified right there in Nauela, and although there was one area where there threatened to be a split among the leaders, the elders reported that the majority of believers throughout the whole district were doing well.

When it was all over and time to climb into the Landrover for the first lap of the journey back to Johannesburg, Gordon and Katie found it very, very hard to say goodbye. These were their people in a special way, and as their eyes passed from one to another of the familiar faces – Maria, Barnardo, Alfonso, Alfreda, Martinho, Jose – they felt as though they were parting from their own children.

But especially Martinho...

12

Crises for Martinho

Martinho was feeling apprehensive. He was conscious
that dark clouds were gathering over the horizon of the
future, and that the comparative peacefulness of church
affairs over the past few years was unlikely to continue.
That era was coming to a close.

By and large, things had gone fairly smoothly since
the memorable opening of the church buildings in
Eleve. The Portuguese authorities seemed to have
accepted it as the visible centre of the congregations
scattered throughout northern Mozambique. They had
even responded to the protestations of parents who did
not want to send their children to the Roman Catholic
school, and had allowed the Protestant school connected with the church at Eleve to function unopposed.
With 500 pupils it was now a flourishing centre of
education, with a commendable record of pupils who
had passed their final exams with high grades.

Things had not always been easy for the congregations in more remote regions, and there had been the
usual incidents of local oppression here and there. One
such event had been the arrival of a policeman with
official authority to smash up the little prayer house at
Ilole, who had proceeded to do so with gusto, ignoring
the protests of Martinho, who happened to be there at
the time. The policeman had barely escaped what

would have been self-inflicted injury when the beams
fell more quickly than he had anticipated, and he had
leapt aside only just in time to avoid them. It gave him a
bit of a shock, since something warned him that it might
have been an act of judgment on the part of The Great
Spirit, and when, that same afternoon, he slipped over
and fractured his arm, his conscience told him it was the
just punishment for his sins. Pain of body was coupled
with anguish of mind. The outcome of that affair had
been the repentance and conversion of the policeman,
who was later baptised and became a church member.
Not all cases of opposition and deliberate persecution
had ended so satisfactorily, of course, but Martinho was
not altogether surprised when it happened. He was
doing God's work, and he was fully assured that God
would work with him.

All the same, he was under no illusions that
everything would be plain sailing now that Frelimo was
in control. Independence Day on 25 June, 1975, had
passed off jubilantly, and had come about more
peaceably than might have been expected, with the
Portuguese eventually pulling out quietly. (The adverse
economic effects of some 200,000 of them leaving the
country with their skills and their equipment was not yet
apparent.) The 500 school children from the Protestant
School in Eleve had been invited to come to the great
gathering of rejoicing in Nauela, and their lusty singing
had been received with warm acclamation. No one
seemed to object to the fact that they sang Christian
hymns. But now disturbing news was coming from
Maputo, the capital, in the far south of the country.
Roman Catholic institutions were coming under attack
as the Marxist Government asserted that religion, and
in particular the Catholic Church, had contributed
powerfully to the oppression of Mozambicans under the
former Portuguese regime. This was being followed by
criticism of such Protestant institutions as existed in the

country, which were pronounced as reactionary and relatively useless. It was being made very clear that under the new constitution Mozambique was a secular state with no religious ties. Its citizens, irrespective of sex, education, occupation or anything else, had equal rights and duties, and although all were free to practise religion, they were also free not to practise religion.

Free not to practise religion. This freedom of non-belief was to be specially safe-guarded. Children's minds must not be corrupted – so Sunday schools must no longer function, and the giving of religious instruction, even to one's own children, was forbidden. There must be no proselytising anywhere. Preaching religion must be confined to the buildings duly registered for that purpose.

'No one must go from village to village to make people religious. We will not permit this,' said Samora Machel, the new President. 'Only Frelimo must do this sort of mobilising . . .'

So what would it all lead to? There was an uneasy atmosphere in the neighbourhood of Nauela now – indeed, in the whole of north Mozambique. The shout of freedom from foreign oppression was subsiding, and a rather ominous quietness taking its place, as news filtered through from one source after another of properties in the south being confiscated, of people being arrested, of some disappearing altogether with no explanation given as to where – or why – or how.

As Martinho knew, the same thing could happen to him and his possessions – and what was even more important, to church possessions. He felt a special sense of responsibility for church possessions, since they belonged to God, who had entrusted them to him and the other elders.

Martinho's was a very uncomplicated attitude towards life. God's work and God's affairs came first, no matter what else was involved, and that simplified

things for him. When he heard of the confiscation of
property, and that Roman Catholic churches and
missions were in the first line of attack, he wondered how
soon Protestant properties would be taken over, too, and
this thoughts flew to the church and the cluster of
church buildings around it at Eleve. He knew there was
nothing he could do to safeguard that property or the
motor that provided the electricity for the buildings, or
the motor cycles used for itinerations. They weren't easy
to hide, and everyone knew of their existence. But
money was a different matter. The church funds in his
possession came to mind, and he decided to secrete
them, along with a few other small but valuable items,
in the church.

It was well that he did so, for when the storm broke in
Nauela, a few months after Independence Day, that
little hoard was practically all that escaped the
'nationalisation' that swept everything before it. All the
church buildings, with the exception of the church itself,
were taken over by the State. (The reason given for this
rather remarkable omission was that it had been built
by the people, for the people, without any foreign funds
or influence.)

Writing of it later, it was typical of Martinho that he
did not fail to give the good, as well as the bad news. He
wanted Senhor Legg to know that however dark the
picture might appear, things were progressing well
spiritually.

'Over Easter weekend, 258 were baptised, 600 were at
the Lord's table, and over 1,000 attended other
meetings,' he wrote in his letter. 'We give thanks to God
who helps us in His work. The elders and leaders remain
united. God gives His power through prayer that we
may be true and faithful believers.' Then he continued
with the more sobering facts, unembellished by
comment.

'I write to inform you that our mission at Eleve has

become the 'Educational Centre', and the school is in
the control of the Government. The things which
belonged to the mission, this includes the motor cycle,
the Bible School, now closed, the clinic and the day
school, and all other buildings have been taken over by
the Frelimo Government...'

What it meant to Martinho and the other church
elders in Eleve, Gordon well understood. History was
being repeated. Just as the mission in Mihecani had
been peremptorily closed by order of the Portuguese
Government, so the mission in Eleve had been closed,
equally peremptorily, by order of Frelimo. He knew
how he and Katie had felt on that never-to-be-forgotten
day when they drove away from Mihecani, the place
that had been the centre of their lives and activities for
years. It had been like having the very ground cut away
from under them, leaving them without a foothold. Now
Martinho and the other elders would be feeling the same
about Eleve, as suddenly there was no school to be
responsible for, no Bible training centre for evangelists,
no clinic with its male nurse...

'Teacher Zefanias has returned to Maputo.' That
brief statement conveyed far more than the information
it contained. The periodical visits of well educated men
like Teacher Zefanias and Pastor Matsombe from the
Baptist churches in the south had raised the academic
standards and been an encouragement in the schools in
Eleve. Now they must cease. And who could tell how
those brothers in Christ were faring?

Such news as came through to Gordon did little to
allay his anxiety. Churches were being closed, Bibles
confiscated, priests and pastors were imprisoned or
simply disappeared. And as month succeeded month
with no further letter from Martinho, all he had to go on
were rumours and the occasional contact with those
who had first-hand information of what was going on in
the district of Nauela.

His own circumstances were congenial enough. His term in office as General Director of the A.E.F. was over, and after eight months of deputation work among churches in Brazil, where an interest was being created in Mozambique, he and Katie had elected not to retire, but to remain in Johannesburg and help in the work among the miners. On one occasion he was greeted with excitement by two of the men in a hostel he was visiting, as they recognised him as their own former missionary in Mihecani. The delight at meeting was mutual. 'We had them in our home one Sunday. After a little meeting and a good meal, I took them back to their hostel, full of gratitude. One of them is particularly keen for the Lord.' Of another occasion he wrote:

'After returning from a visit to a mine this Sunday afternoon, where hundreds of Gospel leaflets were distributed, Katie and I relaxed over a cup of tea,' he added, 'and our conversation covered the past, present and future. It was somewhat startling to realise that our total years of missionary service added up to 81!' And although they had worked in several other countries, there was no doubt as to the one that had left the deepest impressions on their hearts and minds. They were always on the alert to hear any news that came from Mozambique, and especially from the Nauela area, although it was not until a long time afterwards that they heard of the events of 26th July 1976, a date that Martinho himself was never likely to forget. In the afternoon of that day Frelimo soldiers arrived at his house, entered it, and took control of everything. 'They slept in my house, ate my food, stole from my garden, and stayed for a month. They nationalised my table, chairs, cooking pots, dishes, plates, my chickens and goats . . . everything.'

How he and his wife recovered from this devastation of their property Gordon and Katie did not know. Family ties are very strong in Africa, and they could

guess how the couple managed to get started again, with
the help of relatives. Martinho was too occupied and
harassed to write, for calls were reaching him from
places in the province of Niassa and Nampula from
Christians who were being confronted by the Frelimo
authorities and threatened with imprisonment if they
continued teaching their children to believe in God, or if
they were even found with Christian books in their
possession. In some places the little prayer houses were
burnt down, along with any Bibles that could be found.
It was a time of much suffering, and as Martinho
reported later, Frelimo pressure caused many people to
leave Christianity. But in spite of all the oppression, he
continued visiting the various congregations as best he
could, sometimes on foot, sometimes by bicycle,
sometimes by mechanised transport when diesel was
available. And two years after Independence Day he
was urged to visit an area in Nampula province where
he was told there were people wanting to be baptised. So
off he went, and on presenting his travel permit to the
local Administrator, he was asked why he had come.

'I've come to baptise some people who have become
believers, and have asked for it', he replied.

'Baptise people? In the river? Don't you know we've
had no rain for three years, and the river is practically
dry?' was the rather contemptuous comment.

'God will undertake for us', said Martinho, and went
off to call the Christians together to pray. It did not
occur to them that there was any other way of being
baptised but in a river, like the Lord Jesus in the river
Jordan. And since there was not enough water in the
river for them to be properly baptised, the obvious thing
to do was to pray that rain would come. So that is what
they prayed for, and the rain came. The downpour that
night was so great that the river was flooded, and part of
the Administration property was damaged. The
Administrator sent for Martinho and told him to stop

praying immediately – surely there was enough water now!

However, Gordon did not hear about this, or a lot of the happenings of that period, until years later. It would have been sufficiently difficult for Martinho to communicate with Senhor Legg even if there had been only the claims of the churches to respond to. But there were other claims to be met, and they were very time-consuming, to say the least. The Department for Religious Affairs demanded monthly as well as annual reports of what was going on. The Department wanted the names of all pastors and evangelists, notification of any visitors, what they did, where they went, what they said and how long they stayed. Attendances at all registered buildings were to be reported, names of any who were baptised recorded. If any literature was distributed, other than that produced by Frelimo, it was confiscated and destroyed, and the distributors themselves punished.

Visits to Administrators, and long periods of answering questions, were all too often made the more harrowing for Martinho by the knowledge of fellow Christians suffering imprisonment, and possibly torture, and the ever-present threat of the same thing happening to him. And there were always Frelimo indoctrination classes which must be attended, even when they were deliberately held, as was usually the case, at the same time as church services. It was not surprising that for almost a year Gordon received no letter from Martinho until one arrived, late in 1977, asking for Bibles and hymnbooks to be sent, and assuring him that:

'We continue to be firm in the faith in Jesus Christ, just as it was long ago.'

How to obtain the Bibles and hymnbooks in the Lomwe language (there was always a shortage of such literature), and when obtained, how to get them across the border and into Mozambique presented Gordon with an almost insurmountable problem, but the joy of receiving that letter was one of the highlights of his year. And about the same time it was added to by the arrival in one of the mine-hostels he visited, of one of Martinho's own sons.

What excitement! Jose Campos was one of the babies Katie had delivered in the little maternity hospital in Mihecani, and he was able to give them a more intimate picture of his parents' circumstances than ever appeared in Martinho's own letters. Yes, they were in fairly good health, and managing to live on their garden produce. They only had three hens now, and one goat, but there were good crops of vegetables. He would be sending them something each month from his wages as a mine worker. His father was constantly away from home, visiting the various congregations, who were always turning to him when difficulties arose. The church members continued to subscribe towards his travelling expenses, and feed him while he was with them.

Apart from snippets of news from such sources, little was heard of Martinho after that welcome letter in 1977. Occasionally a brief communication would arrive, usually with a request for Bibles and assurances that the work was growing steadily. However dark was the picture economically and politically, however grim some of the stories coming through of the suffering of the people, it seemed that nothing was quenching the rising tide of spiritual life in the churches of Mozambique.

Meanwhile, the Leggs were facing retirement at last. 'To our amazement and to God's praise, we realise that we have served a total of 92 years, many of them spent in Mozambique, now closed to the Gospel,' they wrote to their friends and supporters in the autumn of 1981, explaining that reservations were made for them on a plane that was due to arrive at Heathrow on 4th November. 'But before that will be the hard task of saying "Farewell" to our fellow workers, black and

white, coloured and Indian, whom we have learned to
love in the Lord Jesus, and to leave the continent of
Africa, probably for the last time.'

Everything went according to plan as far as their
arrangements were concerned, and by Christmas they
were comfortably settled in the retirement flat that had
been provided for them in a village near St. Albans.
However, two points in that letter from Africa later
heeded amendment. Mozambique was not closed to the
Gospel, for the turn of the tide was coming. And they
had not left Africa for the last time.

*   *   *

The 1980s will probably go down in history as the period
when Communist policy, almost worldwide, changed its
attitude towards the capitalistic West. It was, of course,
especially noticeable as the countries of the U.S.S.R.
and China eased their tense relationships with U.S.A.
and her allies, largely for economic and technological
reasons. That smaller countries, like Mozambique, were
acting likewise did not make headline news.

From the point of view of religious leaders, the fact
that doors which had been firmly closed began
cautiously to open was all to the good. Communism
remained atheistic, but was prepared to ease some of the
restrictions which oppressed those who were not.

In Mozambique one very evident reason for the
relaxation was the disturbed state of the country itself.
To the worsening economy was added the threat of civil
war as the rebel force, Renamo, increased its guerilla
activities in the remoter regions. The Government could
not afford to make any more enemies. Rather it needed
to mobilise its citizens to stand together against the
disasters, natural as well as political, that were assailing
it. With heat waves so fierce that in Maputo it was
reported even birds were falling dead to the ground;

with drought over wide areas, and women walking for two days to fill their buckets with water; then with rain pouring down relentlessly, making rivers of mountain streams, washing away roads and bridges, submerging gardens and plantations so that seen from the air it looked as though the sea was covering the land along great stretches of the coast from Maputo to Quelimane; with people in the plains fleeing to the hills, as thousands drowned in the floods; with all this happening, it was no time for Government officials to be involved in tracking down delinquents whose only offence was their religious activities. In fact, since Mozambique needed all the foreign aid it could obtain, and as some of that potential aid was likely to be supplied by religious charities, it was sheer folly to act in such a manner as to antagonise, rather than encourage them.

In December, 1982, President Samora Machel called the leaders of the Muslim, Catholic and Protestant faiths together, and announced that the Government was moderating its position against religion. The co-operation of all faiths to combat the problem of the country was needed.

Although that announcement marked the official relaxation of active opposition to religion, the change of attitude had been coming about for some time. This had been noted by the leaders of the Africa Evangelical Fellowship, in which changes had also been taking place. The headquarters in Johannesburg, South Africa, had been closed, an International Headquarters established in the United Kingdom, and a new position of International Director created. As early as 1981 Dr. Robert Foster, International Director, had made a brief visit to Maputo, and the outcome of that visit was recorded later in the words:

'He was encouraged to believe that things were changing in Mozambique, and that the Government's attitude was different. He learned that pastoral visits were possible and was encouraged to send someone to visit the Christians in the north, where A.E.F. missionaries formerly worked.' Then followed the announcement.

'Gordon Legg, now retired, was asked if he would consider a six week visit to the churches in the Zambesia and Nampula areas, where he had worked twenty years before.'

So it came about that less than a year after 'leaving Africa for the last time' Gordon was back, standing in the airport at Maputo and hearing an official saying,

'Senhor Legg, here is your passport. And here is your visa. You have been granted a 50-day visa for your pastoral visit.' Then, as he passed through the barrier, he saw waiting for him Pastor Matsombe of the United Baptists, along with some thirty other African Christians. And among them, standing quietly smiling, but with eyes moistened by tears, was Martinho.

Twelve years, with very differing experiences, had passed since they met for the opening ceremonies of the church at Eleve, but as Gordon hurried forward, arms outstretched, to greet him, they seemed to melt away, and the two of them were back on exactly the same basis on which they had parted. To Gordon, it was like a dream that had come true.

They travelled together, with Pastor Matsombe, for six or seven weeks – weeks that seemed crammed with unforgettable experiences. Travel for thirteen hours in a railway carriage holding 140 others was almost as perturbing as riding on a 27-year-old truck with no brakes, no lights, a leaky radiator and worn-out gears. But such inconveniences sank into insignificance when compared with the excitement and amazement at what Martinho told him, and what he saw with his own eyes of the work of God in Mozambique, particularly in the northern areas he knew so well.

'All that I heard and saw caused me to give thanks to

God for what He had done. There has been a terrific multiplication in the number of churches, now over 400, a tenfold increase in 21 years. There are 44,000 baptised believers, according to official statistics which were forwarded to the Government at the beginning of 1982. There are 87 pastors (men with the hearts of shepherds), and 1,171 evangelists and church leaders.

'It was thrilling to be amongst these Christians again. Some meetings were small, but others had as many as 1,800 present. What excitement! What clapping of hands and singing! What messages of welcome everywhere! There were many loving gifts, even out of their poverty.' The poverty was almost alarming in some districts, where cloth for clothing had not been available for years. Some were reduced to wearing garments made out of woven plastic sacks, bark rope and natural fibre. Yet what they had they were willing to give – an egg, a few potatoes, vegetables dug up from their little gardens.

'What a privilege to be entrusted with the ministry of the Word to such people! Many young peoples' groups sang their pieces with such fervour and meaning – it was very encouraging to see so many between the ages of 18–25. It speaks well for the future. Pray that they may keep true to their Lord. The devil knows of this increase, too, and will not let it go unchallenged.

'The eagerness and hunger for the Word of God was unparalleled in my experience,' he reported when it was all over, and he was home again. 'One of the greatest needs is that these leaders, over 1,000 of them, who have had little opportunity to learn the things of God and are eager to know more, might get a fuller grasp of basic doctrines of the faith. Both Pastor Matsombe and Pastor Martinho Campos are asking our help to re-establish a Bible training programme at Eleve and in Maputo. There is a great dearth of Bibles, hymn books and study books in Portuguese, and the two million Lomwe-

Makus people in the north have only the New
Testament and Psalms in their own language.

'There are near famine conditions in many areas, and
general unrest and guerilla warfare. Bandit gangs and
raids on villages. The pastors had their motor cycles
confiscated years ago, and the evangelists have no
bicycles. Yet they still get around as best they can...'
He found it hard to go on with his report sometimes,
remembering the voluntary evangelists with their
threadbare trousers and tattered shirts, setting off bare-
foot, smiles on their faces, to walk through the bush to
some village or cluster of houses miles away. His
memories obviously moved him deeply, and those who
listened to his report could not fail to be touched. But
they were not merely touched. When he urged, 'The
open door of opportunity calls us to immediate action,'
the response was unanimous. The time had come to
move forward.

'The A.E.F. now faces the greatest challenge and
opportunity for many years,' wrote Dr. Robert Foster
later, as he publicly announced the launching of Project
Mozambique.

'First let us bow in worship and praise to God for all
He has done in establishing a vigorous, thriving church
in northern Mozambique,' he wrote, going on to outline
the Fellowship's goals for 1983. They included the
calling of three missionary couples for Bible teaching, a
Bible translator, the supply of thousands of hymnbooks
and Bibles, fifty bicycles for evangelists to use, and a
Landrover for the Superintendent's visits throughout
the whole of north Mozambique.

And since the whole project required an experienced
co-ordinator, one with an intimate knowledge of the
country who was fluent in Portuguese, Gordon Legg
was asked to serve as 'Secretary for Mozambique'.

*   *   *

There was an added reason for communication between
Gordon and Martinho now. Their official positions, one
as Secretary for Mozambique, the other as Superintendent of the United Baptist Churches in the north,
required it of them. Martinho kept Gordon as fully
informed as possible about conditions, although it was
probably the visit of Dr. Foster himself to Nauela in
1984 that provided the more vivid picture. He admitted
that in all his many years of missionary experiences in
Africa he had seen nothing like it.

'The joy, enthusiasm and generosity of the believers
who have suffered so much, and have so little, was
utterly incredible. It reminded me time and again of the
early Church in the opening chapters of Acts ... In one
area the number of churches has multiplied so fast that
there were not enough New Testaments in Lomwe to go
round. So what did they do? They divided one into
separate books and shared a book or two with each
group. After a month they passed them on, and so it
continued until each church had had the opportunity to
read the whole New Testament.

'The lack of hymn books hasn't kept the Christians
from singing. Everywhere we went we were treated to
original hymns and tunes created by the people
themselves.' But that was not all that impressed Dr.
Foster. 'With no clothing available for years, many now
are reduced to wearing garments made out of woven
plastic sacks and bark rope. Time and time again we
were appalled by the fact that neither church leaders
nor people had any blankets to sleep in at nights.
Hardship and suffering are everyday experiences, yet
their joy in the Lord and their triumph over circumstances has left an indelible impression on my heart, so
that I can never be quite the same again.'

He wanted to send them a thousand blankets as soon
as possible, just as a tangible evidence of love, but that
was only to be a beginning. Bicycles, Bibles, a Land-

rover . . . But still there was more that could be done in a
practical way to help those believers in Mozambique, so
in addition to writing to Portugal and Brazil for Bibles
and study courses, Gordon started exploring ways of
getting food and clothes sent to them.

The following year he visited Mozambique again,
and this time Katie was with him. Of the fortnight they
spent in Nampula, he rather humorously observed that
he had never seen Katie kissed so much. A number of the
women they met had either given birth to children in
her maternity department at Mihecani, or had been
born there themselves, as had many of the men, who had
also received their education in the school. 'So we were
among friends. We lived in African homes, where we
received much love and kindness. There were over 900
present at the first Sunday service, and in African style
we shook hands with them all as they left.' It was a tiring
but a thrilling time for them, and they returned to
England with an inspiring story to tell of the growth and
health of the Church.

But there was a dark side to the picture, too. General
conditions in Mozambique had proved far worse than
they had anticipated.

'Armed bandits roam the rural areas, committing
atrocities, killing women and children, taking their
cattle and personal belongings, even within a few miles
of major cities. One pastor in the south has not slept in
his house for two years, but each night takes his family to
sleep under the trees for fear of armed brigands. Another
pastor died from hunger when his area was surrounded
by brigands, and relief could not get through in time.'

City shops boarded up as there was nothing to sell.
Bread queues forming overnight, in the hope of
obtaining bread in the morning. Rice rationed, and so
inadequate that the last two weeks of every month there
was widespread hunger. What was perhaps even worse
were the inroads being made by Renamo. How many of

the bands of ruthless men roaming the countryside were actually members of the rebel force, and how many were armed bandits it was difficult to say, but they were on the increase. People were in terror of them, for no one knew where they would strike next.

Then came the news that the Renamo had arrived in Nauela. That they had surrounded the area around Eleve. And that among those who had been killed was Pastor Martinho Campos.

13

'If God be for us . . .'

Martinho was in the Landrover on his way back from visiting one of the more distant congregations when he heard that the Renamo were advancing on Nauela. It was as he was getting near home that he saw coming towards him on the road three men with their families, laden with bundles and pots and pans, whom he recognised as being shopkeepers who lived not far from him. The Landrover came to a halt as he leaned out to enquire where they were going.

'The Renamo are coming!' they told him breathlessly. 'They are surrounding Nauela . . .'

So the Renamo were actually advancing at last! He knew they had been entrenched a hundred or so miles away for months, though their acts of reckless violence had terrorised neighbourhoods over a far wider area. There had been the burning of four large warehouses of grain not far from Nauela that had appalled and baffled the authorities as they gazed helpless at the blaze which destroyed food enough to feed thousands of people for months. One never knew where 'the armed bandits' would strike next. And when they arrived suddenly at some isolated group of dwellings, one never knew what they would do. Martinho had heard some horrifying reports in the course of his travels. Young Christian women whom he knew personally had been promptly

shot dead when they refused to accede to the immoral
demands of the bandits who burst into their homes. He
had been told explicitly of four such cases, and knew
there were many more. Men, too, were liable to be
'executed' on the slightest pretext.

Ernesto, one of the evangelists, had had a narrow
escape when confronted by a group of armed men who
burst into his house and accused him of being a spy for
the Government. They refused to believe that his travels
had merely been in connection with the church, and he
felt his last hour had come as he emptied his pockets of
what papers they contained, and saw the threatening
expression on his captors' faces. But then a snapshot fell
out of the tattered notebook in which he kept his
records. It was a snapshot of Gordon Legg. One of the
men snatched it up, looked at it, and said:

'I know this white man.' Then he looked at Ernesto
and said, 'You must be a preacher, eh?' 'That's just
what I've been telling you,' replied Ernesto, and the
man gave a little nod. 'So they let me go,' said Ernesto,
relating the incident later, and he added, 'That
snapshot saved my life!'

But there had been others who had not escaped, and
Martinho well knew that as a leader in his own area, he
would be a marked man when the Renamo arrived. He
looked at the little group of people standing by him in
the road, saw the fearful expressions on their faces,
heard the pleading note in the voice of one of the men as
he said:

'Oh, Martinho, will you help us? Will you give us a lift
in your Landrover back to the town? We'll be safe there.
It's such a long way for the children to walk, and if the
Renamo catch up with us . . . Oh, Martinho, help us!'

The decision had to be made then and there, and
Martinho took the action that nearly cost him his life.
He turned the Landrover, drove the little group to the
nearest town, then set off as quickly as he could for his

home in Eleve.

He was arrested by the Renamo commander shortly
after he arrived, and brought to trial. The accusation
made against him was that he had helped men who were
due for execution to escape. He had met them on the
road and taken them off to the town. He was threatened
with death himself then, but replied that he was not
afraid to die, as he would go straight to Heaven and be
with the Lord Jesus. After a week the Renamo officials
decided not to kill him, but to put him under house
arrest instead, and confiscate the Landrover.

It has been said that three of the component virtues
that make up manliness are resolution, courage and
fortitude. Of Martinho's resolution there had been no
question. He had decided to be a servant of Jesus Christ,
and had never swerved from that. His courage had been
tested when he was faced with the realisation that going
on deliberately into an area being taken over by the
Renamo was running inevitably into personal danger.
He might have turned back and sought refuge in the
town, like those he had helped to escape. But more than
anything else fortitude was what was called for in the
months that lay ahead of him now. The pathway was to
be one of suffering.

He had been under house arrest for nearly a year
without any knowledge of what would happen to him
when one day there was a great bustle in the yard, with
much coming and going, and occasionally the sound of
firing. Then he was brought out, along with scores of
other prisoners, some of whom he recognised. There
were, in fact, about a hundred and twenty men
altogether, who had been specially selected because
they were religious leaders in some faith or other.
Among them he saw Muslims, Roman Catholics as well
as Protestants. They were to be taken to Renamo
headquarters for questioning about their religions.

So the march started. There were twenty men and
officers, well armed, in charge, and their aim was

evidently to push the prisoners as hard as they could, to their destination. They had to walk. Whatever arrangements had been made for the physical needs of the guards did not extend to the prisoners. The only food they got was what the solders snatched from villagers whose homes and gardens they passed, and handed on to them. They were roused roughly at dawn, got into line, and told to move in the direction indicated. They trudged on from morning till night, when they sank on the ground to get what rest they could until the march started again. It was nineteen days before they reached Murumbala, the Renamo headquarters.

'We arrived beaten, crushed, exhausted', Martinho reported later. 'We suffered greatly, walking on foot in the interior of thick bush, only sleeping in the bush with nothing to eat. The object of all this was for them to know the characteristics of each church and what each religious body taught. We told them everything.'

Under threat of death the Renamo tried to persuade them to change faith and join their Zionist church. For the Renamo, too, were religionists. Their faith was a perplexing mixture of Christianity and African animism, its religious activity taking the form, as Martinho expressed it, of 'praying, dancing, and beating drums.' The Zionist church, they claimed, would be the national church once Renamo had gained the total victory. Not surprisingly, their persuasions and threats failed completely where Martinho was concerned, and after about ten days he was allowed to return to Nauela, along with some others, again under guard.

But this journey proved too much for him. His legs were swollen, his feet like pulp, and after two weary weeks he was too exhausted to stagger on any further. The proddings and shoutings of the soldiers had no effect. He just lay where he had tripped over, unable to move.

He was not the first one to fall like that. A fellow evangelist, suffering from acute asthma, had collapsed

and died a week earlier, and been hurriedly buried in
the sand by fellow prisoners. When Martinho fell and
could not rise, they decided to leave him to die and went
on, leaving a few of the stragglers behind to bury him
when he died. The depleted contingent of prisoners
eventually reached Nauela, where the non-appearance
of Martinho gave rise to the rumour that he had been
shot by the side of the road.

The rumour was accepted without question. There
seemed no reason to doubt it. Gordon first heard of it in
a letter from Martinho's own son-in-law in Portugal.
Then it came to A.E.F. headquarters from the General
Superintendent of the Baptist churches in Maputo.

'Leaders like him are rare in any community and his
loss will be felt deeply in Mozambique', wrote Dr.
Foster in a news release dated 23 September, 1986. The
news was circulated throughout the A.E.F., and articles
about Martinho's life and service, and his supposed
death at the hands of the Renamo, appeared in
Christian magazines. His loss was certainly felt, and five
months later no one had been appointed to take his
place as Superintendent in north Mozambique. Then,
quite suddenly, a public announcement from Quelimane was received in Maputo. It read:

I wish to make it known to all the Christian brothers of
the Igreja Uniao Baptists de Moçambique, Pastors,
Evangelists,   Deacons,   Youth   Leaders,   that   I,
MARTINHO CAMPOS, the Regional Superintendent
of the I.U.B. de M., am well by the mercy of God, and
am in the pastoral ministry in Quelimane. I wish to ask
all the brothers in Christ that we ought faithfully to
continue following the Word of God, walking worthily,
pleasing our God in everything, in a true and abundant
life, in brotherly love of our Lord Jesus Christ. Amen.
                Quelimane, 10th February 1987
        The Regional Superintendent of I.U.B.M.
                MARTINHO CAMPOS.

On the same day Martinho wrote a letter to Senhor
Gordon Legg in England. It started with the words:

'I give thanks to God, the Creator of heaven and
earth, who by His mercy has kept me in days of distress,
when I did not expect to live. Our God is faithful to all
who ask, and He hears their prayers so that I, Martinho
Campos, am alive by the love of our Saviour Jesus
Christ . . .

'During this past year I have been at Nauela. On the
5th and 6th of April 1986 the armed bandits surrounded
the Nauela area, making it impossible to leave or enter,
and it was impossible to write letters. For 10 months I
was in captivity and suffered greatly.

'On 9th June, 1986 they made all religious people and
leaders of all religions to go to Murumbala, their
headquarters, a very long journey on foot.' Then he
went on to describe briefly what happened there, and
how they set out on the return journey.

'Now on the way I fell gravely ill, and my feet were
crushed, like pulp, so was unable to walk also with my
bad rheumatism, and of course no medicines, I was
exhausted. One day I stopped in the middle of the
desert, and there I remained for two weeks . . .' He had
not been expected to live, but although he and the few
others left with him had neither food nor shelter, they
managed to survive on what berries and roots they could
find. After about a fortnight Martinho had recovered
enough strength to walk a few steps, then stop, then walk
again. It was slow progress, 'but little by little I walked
for another month, then I arrived at Nauela, thanking
God. It was this that caused me to suffer so much,' he
wrote, but went on more cheerfully, 'Now I am
continuing in the work of God. This continues
developing strongly by His power. We have now in
Nauela 53 churches because we opened new places and
the work of God has not stopped. Thursdays women
meet for prayer. Sundays we have worship services,
instruction classes, Sunday school. The young people

sing their hymns and have music. All is running well, in spite of how much we have suffered, and we have gained strength to evangelise with the Word of God.'

But as 1987 dawned another change took place. The Frelimo forces broke through the Renamo encirclement and regained control of Nauela. The Frelimo commander, finding Martinho Campos and three priests still in Nauela, decided to take them to Quelimane to be interviewed by the Governor. 'On February 10th we went to see His Excellency. All went well. I was received by Frelimo, and given a permit to travel and continue in the work of the Lord.' So that is how it came about.

He was free at last to communicate with his colleagues and his friends, and he lost no time in doing so. He intended continuing his pastoral visits to the churches, he told Gordon, even down to Maputo if necessary, and mentioned the need for Bibles and hymn books. It was quite a businesslike letter in some ways, giving a report to the man he still looked to as his counsellor as well as his friend. Only at the end of it did he give expression to any personal needs or desires. One of these was almost in the form of an apologetic postscript, 'Forgive me please, I do not know how I can possibly ask you for vitamin tablets. But I need them badly.' Gordon and Katie lost no time in sending a good supply to him.

The other desire was not so easy of fulfilment, as far as they were concerned. 'I would very much like to see you and your wife. I do not know in what way.' They did not know in what way, either. They read the words again: 'I would very much like to see you and your wife. I do not know in what way.' But then Martinho continued, 'God knows. Let us pray to God to open the way, that I might come to meet you.'

And God, whose tender mercies are over all His works, and whose understanding is infinite, heard and answered that prayer. Martinho received an earnest invitation from the International Director of the Africa

Evangelical Fellowship to come to England, not only to visit International Headquarters in Reading, but also to spend some days with the Secretary for Mozambique, Mr. Gordon Legg, and his wife in their home near St. Albans.

* * *

If the ten days Martino spent with Senhor Legg and Dona Caterina in the autumn of 1987 was the fulfilment of his heart's desire, the same could be said for them. It was five years since Gordon had met him, and even longer in Katie's case, yet no one else could ever take his place. Quite apart from the personal affection they had for him, he was the living link between them and the people among whom they had lived so long in Nauela. Reminiscences of the past were brought to life again as he gave up to date news of this one and that one, told them of being called to place after place to examine new applicants for baptism. He had so much to tell them.

What was happening was beyond himself and his own activities. Martinho was convinced of that. Hearts were prepared in such a way that the message of the love of God as revealed in Jesus Christ found an immediate response. It was like a seed that fell into good ground – ground that had been softened by suffering, fertilised by shame and humiliation. When he spoke of the work of God and the power of God, he was speaking of something that could not be defined or analysed in human terms, and Martinho did not attempt to do so. All he knew was that the Most High God was moving in power in the people of his country, and for some reason he himself could not understand, God had called him to be a co-worker. He had no other thought beyond serving his Master. And as Gordon and Katie listened to what he had to tell them of the earnestness and faith of the leaders, the fervent desire for Bible knowledge, the generosity of the believers who gave so willingly out of the depth of their poverty, they marvelled at what God was doing in the land that was suffering so much.

For there was no doubt about the suffering. Drought and famine were affecting millions of people, and towns were crowded with refugees, while thousands had fled over the borders into neighbouring countries. Martinho had some horrifying stories to tell of the brutality and violence of the armed bandits, robbing terrified women and children as well as men of the very clothes they were wearing. Nakedness as well as hunger cried out for help from Mozambique and Gordon was glad he could tell Martinho about the great containers full of good second-hand clothing that had been shipped out there, seven of them from northern Ireland. He hoped that more would soon be on the way.

Martinho's visit culminated in two or three days at International Headquarters, where matters were discussed relating to the opportunities for A.E.F. workers to go out to co-operate with the Church, especially in Bible teaching. Five were there already, and looking back to the time when Mihecani was closed, and he and Katie had driven off in their Landrover, their only home, Gordon remembered that at that time it had looked as though the curse of King Lion was being fulfilled, with the messengers of Jesus Christ being driven out of the land. But God had turned the curse into a blessing. Greater fruitfulness had been experienced after they left than when they were there. And now the door that had seemed to be permanently closed was opening again. How wide it would open, and how long it would remain so, was something neither he nor anyone else could foretell. While the opportunity lasted, it must be grasped, and he was thankful that he could still have a share in it.

Gordon had not left Africa for the last time. When he saw Martinho off at Heathrow, he did so quite cheerfully, for he was scheduled to go out himself for four weeks, early in the following year. And as Martinho turned his head to smile his goodbye before passing through the Passengers Only barrier, they knew they would meet again – in Mozambique.

EPILOGUE

by Dr Robert Frost

What of the future?

As 1988 draws to a close the country of Mozambique is still ravaged by civil war, and much of the countryside out of bounds. With hundreds of thousands displaced from their homes and many thousands more refugees in neighbouring lands, famine continues to stalk the land. The economic plight of this beautiful country and its people is reckoned to be one of the worst on the face of the earth. In spite of generous aid from many countries the end of the conflict and turmoil is not in sight.

However, the other side of the picture is much brighter. The Church of Jesus Christ continues to grow and multiply. The Igreja União Baptista, which had its origins in the south at Maputo and in the north at Mihecani, has spread today to every province of the country. Church membership numbers at least 160,000 and the work continues to grow. During this past year many new churches have been formed, even among the Muslim peoples of the north.

The hunger for the Word of God is incredible, and trained leadership for the churches is an absolute priority. The Evangelical Seminary of Mozambique has been opened in temporary quarters in Maputo, sponsored by the Igreja União Baptista and the Africa Evangelical Fellowship. Land has been donated by the government and construction has begun. Training is being provided on several educational levels to prepare men and women for leadership in the church.

The cry for more training centres and programmes comes from every part of the country, particularly the north. Missionaries qualified to teach the Word and train leadership are urgently needed today, and the government is willing to grant visas to such workers.

The seed was planted by Gordon Legg and others of his generation. Through expulsion of the missionary and closure of the work, God has brought new life and an abundant harvest. Through subsequent persecution following independence and the guerrilla war Christians have been scattered to every corner of the country and new churches planted. God is at work!

As we look into the future, the great challenge that faces us today is to train men and women in the Word of God so that they are rooted and grounded in the truth. Then the church will continue to stand in the years that lie ahead. Where are the Gordons and the Martinhos?

Will you pray that God will call and send forth qualified disciples? Will you enable someone to go? Will you go?

THE AFRICA EVANGELICAL FELLOWSHIP

The AEF is an international evangelical mission. For more information about their work please contact them at their International Office, 17 Westcote Road, Reading, Berks RG3 2DL.

The AEF has hundreds of opportunities for both long and short term service in evangelism, church planting, education, medical administration, youth work and other practical fields.

Other AEF Offices are:

Australia
PO Box 292
Castle Hill
New South Wales 2154

Canada:
470 McNicoll Avenue
Willowdale
Ontario M2H 2E1

USA:
PO Box 2896
Boone
North Carolina 28607

UK:
30 Lingfield Road
Wimbledon
London SW19 4PU

Zimbabwe:
99 Gaydon Road
Graystone Park
Borrowdale
Harare

South Africa:
Rowland House
6 Montrose Avenue
Claremont 7700

New Zealand:
PO Box 1390
Invercargill

European:
5 Rue de Meautry
94500 Campigny-Sur-Marne
France